PHRASEBOOK
PORTUGUESE

PHRASEBOOK   AA
PORTUGUESE

English edition prepared by First Edition Translations Ltd,
Great Britain
Designed and produced by AA Publishing
First published in 1995 as Wat & Hoe Portugees,
© Uitgeverij Kosmos bv - Utrecht/Antwerpen
Van Dale Lexicografie bv - Utrecht/Antwerpen
This edition © Automobile Association Developments Limited 2005
Reprinted September 2008

A CIP catalogue record for this book is available from the
British Library.

Published by AA Publishing (a trading name of Automobile
Association Developments Limited, whose registered office is
Fanum House, Basingstoke, Hampshire RG21 4EA. Registered
number 1878835).

Typeset by Information Engineers, Cambridge.
Printed and bound in China by Everbest.

Find out more about AA Publishing by visiting our website at
www.theAA.com/bookshop

A03953

Contents

5 On the road 63–81

6 Public transport 82–93

7 Overnight accommodation 94–104

8 Money matters 105–108

9 Post and telephone 109–116

Introduction

● **Welcome to the AA's essential Phrase Books series**, covering the most popular European languages and containing everything you'd expect from a comprehensive language series. They're concise, accessible and easy to understand, and you'll find them indispensable on your trip abroad.

Each guide is divided into 15 themed sections and starts with a pronunciation table which gives you the phonetic spelling to all the words and phrases you'll need to know for your trip, while at the back of the book is an extensive word list and grammar guide which will help you construct basic sentences in your chosen language.

Throughout the book you'll come across coloured boxes with a [symbol] beside them. These are designed to help you if you can't understand what your listener is saying to you. Hand the book over to them and encourage them to point to the appropriate answer to the question you are asking.

Other coloured boxes in the book – this time without the symbol – give alphabetical listings of themed words with their English translations beside them.

For extra clarity, we have put all English words and phrases in black, foreign language terms in brown and their phonetic pronunciation in italic.

This phrase book covers all subjects you are likely to come across during the course of your visit, from reserving a room for the night to ordering food and drink at a restaurant and what to do if your car breaks down or you lose your traveller's cheques and money. With over 2,000 commonly used words and essential phrases at your fingertips you can rest assured that you will be able to get by in all situations, so let the essential Phrase Book become your passport to a secure and enjoyable trip!

Pronunciation table

English speakers can imitate the actual sound of the words by saying the version in italics. Correctly placed stress is essential:
Words ending in a vowel or in **m** or **s** are usually stressed on the penultimate syllable, for example:

o rato   (oo rah-too)   the mouse

Words that end in a consonant other than **m** or **s** are stressed on the last syllable e.g. **cruel** (croo-ell) - cruel, and exceptions to the rule are words marked with an accent, for example, **falência** (bankruptcy).
Emphasised nasal pronunciation is indicated by the til accent (~), for example, **nações** (nations).

Vowels

ã	pronounced approximately as in **sung** (**irmã**)
ão	pronounced as **ow** in **howl** (**limão**)
final e	barely pronounced (**onde**)
ê	as in **they** (**relê**)
es	*sh* as in **Estoril** (shtooreel)
final o	as in **loop** (**macaco**)
ô	as in **local** (**vôo**)
u	as in **rule**, and silent in **gue**, **gui**, **que** and **qui**

Consonants

ç	as in **receive**, e.g. *laço*
ch	as in **shock**, e.g. *choque*
h	always silent, e.g. *hora*
lh	as **ll** in **million**, e.g. *milhão*
nh	as **ni** in **onion**, e.g. *linha*
qu	before **e** or **i** pronounced as in **kick**, e.g. *quilo*; before **a** or **o** pronounced as in **quote**, e.g. *qualidade*
r	always trilled
-s-	before **b, d, g, l, m, n, r** and **v**, as in **leisure** e.g. *rasgo*
-s-, -s	before **c, f, p, qu, t** and when it is the last letter, with a **sh** sound as in **sugar**, e.g. *respeito*
x	initial or before a consonant as pronounced as in **sugar**, e.g. *xícara*; in **ex** pronounced as in **squeeze**, e.g. *exemplo*
z	when in final position, as in **leisure**, e.g. *conduz*, otherwise like an ordinary z

1

Useful lists

1.1 Today or tomorrow?

What day is it today? __	Que dia é hoje?
	kuh deeah eh oarje?
Today's Monday _____	Hoje é segunda-feira
	oarje eh segunda-fayrah
– Tuesday _____	Hoje é terça-feira
	oarje eh tearsah-fayrah
– Wednesday _____	Hoje é quarta-feira
	oarje eh cuartah-fayrah
– Thursday_____	Hoje é quinta-feira
	oarje eh keentah-fayrah
– Friday _____	Hoje é sexta-feira
	oarje eh seshtah-fayrah
– Saturday _____	Hoje é sábado
	oarje eh sarbadoo
– Sunday _____	Hoje é domingo
	oarje eh doomeengoo
in January _____	em Janeiro
	ey janayroo
since February _____	desde Fevereiro
	desduh fevverayroo
in spring_____	na primavera
	nuh preemaverrah
in summer _____	no verão
	noo verau
in autumn_____	no outono
	noo ohtohnoo
in winter _____	no inverno
	noo invairnoo
1997 _____	mil novecentos e noventa e sete
	meel novsentush ee nooventa ee set
the twentieth century___	o século XX (vinte)
	oo seckooloo veent
What's the date today?_	Que dia é hoje?
	kuh deeah eh oarje

Today's the 24th _____	Hoje é dia vinte e quatro
	oarje eh deeah veent ee cuartroo
Monday, November ___ 2nd, 1998	segunda feira, dois de Novembro de 1998
	segunda fayrah, doysh duh novembroo duh meel novsentush ee novventa ee aytoo
in the morning _____	de manhã
	duh manyair
in the afternoon _____	de tarde
	duh tard
in the evening _____	à noite
	ah noyt
at night _____	de noite
	duh noyt
this morning _____	hoje de manhã
	oarje duh manyair
this afternoon _____	hoje à tarde
	oarje ah tard
this evening _____	hoje à noite
	oarje ah noyt
tonight _____	esta noite
	eshta noyt
last night _____	na noite passada
	nah noyt passada
this week _____	esta semana
	eshta semarnah
next month _____	no próximo mês
	noo prossimoo mayge
last year _____	no ano passado
	noo arnoo passardoo
next... _____	no próximo...
	noo prosseemoo...
in...days/weeks/ months/years _____	daqui a...dias/semanas/meses/anos
	dakee ah...deeash/semarnash/ mayzesh/arnoosh

...weeks ago _____ hã...semanas
ah...semarnash
day off _____ feriado
ferriardoo

1.2 Bank holidays

● **The main public holidays** in Portugal are the following:

January 1	Ano Novo (New Year's Day)
February	Carnaval (Carnival)
March/April	Sexta-feira Santa (Good Friday)
April 25	Dia da Revolução (Day of the Revolution)
May 1	Dia do Trabalhador (Labour Day)
June 10	Dia de Portugal (Camões Day commemorating Portugal's equivalent to Shakespeare)
June 13	Santo António (Festival of St Anthony, patron saint of Lisbon)
June 24	São João (Festival of St John, celebrated in Oporto and the North)
August 15	Assunção da Nossa Senhora (Feast of the Assumption)
October 5	Dia da República (Republic Day)
November 1	Dia de Todos os Santos (All Saints Day)
December 1	Restauração da Independência (Restoration Day)
December 8	Imaculada Conceição (Feast of the Immaculate Conception)
December 25	Dio da Nata (Christmas Day)

Most shops, banks and government departments are closed on these days.

Boxing Day is not a public holiday.

1.3 What time is it?

What time is it? _____	Que horas são?
	kay oarash sow?
It's nine o'clock _____	São nove horas
	sow nov oarash
– five past ten _____	São dez e cinco
	sow dez ee seenkoo
– a quarter past eleven _	São onze e um quarto
	sow onz ee oom cuartoo
– twenty past twelve ___	É meio dia e vinte
	eh mayoo deeah ee veent
– half past one _____	É uma e meia
	eh oomah ee mayah
– twenty-five to three __	São três menos vinte e cinco
	sow trayge mennush veent ee seenkoo
– a quarter to four ____	São quatro menos um quarto
	sow cuartroo mennush oom cuartoo
– ten to five _____	São cinco menos dez
	sow seenkoo mennush dej/
– twelve noon _____	É meio dia
	eh mayoo deeah
– midnight _____	É meia noite
	eh mayah noyt
half an hour _____	uma meia hora
	oomah mayah orah
What time? _____	A que horas?
	ah kay orash?
What time can I come __ round?	A que horas é que posso ir?
	ah kay orash eh kuh possoo eer?
At... _____	Às...
	ush...
After... _____	Depois das...
	depoysh dush...
Before... _____	Antes das...
	antesh dush...

Between...and... _____	Entre as...e as...
	entrash...ee ush...
From...to... _____	Das...às...
	dush...ush
In...minutes _____	Daqui a...minutos
	dakee uh...minootoosh
– an hour _____	Daqui a uma hora
	dakee uh ooma ora
– ...hours _____	Daqui a...horas
	dakee uh...orash
– a quarter of an hour __	Daqui a um quarto de hora
	dakee ah oom cuartoo dora
– three quarters of _____	Daqui a três quartos de hora
an hour	*dakee ah trayge cuartoosh dora*
early/late _____	cedo/tarde
	sedoo/tard
on time _____	a horas
	uh orash
summertime _____	horário de verão
	oraryoo duh verau
wintertime _____	horário de inverno
	orarioo duh invairnoo

1.4 One, two, three...

0 _____	zero	*zairoo*
1 _____	um	*oom*
2 _____	dois	*doysh*
3 _____	três	*trayge*
4 _____	quatro	*cuartroo*
5 _____	cinco	*seenkoo*
6 _____	seis	*saysh*
7 _____	sete	*set*
8 _____	oito	*oytoo*
9 _____	nove	*nov*

10	_____	dez	*dej*
11	_____	onze	*onz*
12	_____	doze	*doaze*
13	_____	treze	*treyze*
14	_____	catorze	*cattorz*
15	_____	quinze	*keenze*
16	_____	dezasseis	*dezzasaysh*
17	_____	dezassete	*dezzaset*
18	_____	dezoito	*dezzoytoo*
19	_____	dezanove	*dezzanov*
20	_____	vinte	*veent*
21	_____	vinte e um	*veenty oom*
22	_____	vinte e dois	*veenty doysh*
30	_____	trinta	*treenta*
31	_____	trinta e um	*treenty oom*
32	_____	trinta e dois	*treenty doysh*
40	_____	quarenta	*cuarenta*
50	_____	cinquenta	*seencuenta*
60	_____	sessenta	*sessenta*
70	_____	setenta	*settenta*
80	_____	oitenta	*oytenta*
90	_____	noventa	*nooventa*
100	_____	cem	*same*
101	_____	cento e um	*sentoo ee oom*
110	_____	cento e dez	*sentoo ee dej*
120	_____	cento e vinte	*sentoo ee veent*
200	_____	duzentos	*doozentoosh*
300	_____	trezentos	*trayzentoosh*
400	_____	quatrocentos	*cuartroosentoosh*
500	_____	quinhentos	*keenyentush*
600	_____	seiscentos	*sayshsentoosh*
700	_____	setecentos	*setsentoosh*
800	_____	oitocentos	*oytsentoosh*
900	_____	novecentos	*novsentoosh*
1000	_____	mil	*meel*
1100	_____	mil e cem	*meely same*
2000	_____	dois mil	*doysh meel*

10,000 _____	dez mil	*dej meel*
100,000 _____	cem mil	*say meel*
1,000,000 _____	milhão	*meelyau*
1st _____	primeiro	*preemayroo*
2nd _____	segundo	*seggoondoo*
3rd _____	terceiro	*tairsayroo*
4th _____	quarto	*cuartoo*
5th _____	quinto	*keentoo*
6th _____	sexto	*seshtoo*
7th _____	sétimo	*settimoo*
8th _____	oitavo	*oytahvoo*
9th _____	nono	*nohnoo*
10th _____	décimo	*dessimoo*
11th _____	décimo primeir	*dessimoo preemayroo*
12th _____	décimo segundo	*dessimoo segundoo*
13th _____	décimo terceiro	*dessimoo tairsayroo*
14th _____	décimo quarto	*dessimoo cuartoo*
15th _____	décimo quinto	*dessimoo keentoo*
16th _____	décimo sexto	*dessimoo seshtoo*
17th _____	décimo sétimo	*dessimoo settimoo*
18th _____	décimo oitavo	*dessimoo oytarvoo*
19th _____	décimo nono	*dessimoo nohnoo*
20th _____	vigésimo	*veejezimoo*
21st _____	vigésimo primeiro	*veejezimoo preemayroo*
22nd _____	vigésimo segundo	*veejezimoo segoondoo*
30th _____	trigésimo	*treejezimoo*
100th _____	centésimo	*sentezimoo*
1000th _____	milésimo	*milezimoo*
once _____	uma vez	
	ooma vayzh	
twice _____	duas vezes	
	dooash vayzesh	
double _____	o dobro	
	oo dobroo	

triple	_____	o triplo
		oo treeploo
half	_____	a metade
		uh mettard
a quarter	_____	um quarto
		oom cuartoo
a third	_____	um terço
		oom tairsoo
a couple, a few, some	___	um par de, uns, alguns
		oom par duh, oonsh, algoomash
2+4=6	_____	dois mais quatro são seis
		doysh mysh cuartroo sow saysh
4-2=2	_____	quatro menos dois são dois
		cuartroo mennush doysh sow doysh
2x4=8	_____	dois vezes quatro são oito
		dooash vayzesh cuartroo sow oytoo
4÷2=2	_____	quatro a dividir por dois são dois
		cuartroo uh divvideer por doysh sow doysh
odd/even	_____	par/ímpar
		par/eempar
total	_____	(em) total
		(aim) tootal
6x9	_____	seis por nove
		saysh por nov

1.5 The weather

Is the weather going to be good/bad?	_____	Estará bom/mau tempo?
		estarah bom tempoo?
Is it going to get colder/hotter?	_____	Estará mais frio/calor?
		estarah mysh freeooh/calore?
What temperature is it going to be?	_____	Quantos graus vão estar?
		cuarntoosh growsh vow eshtar?
Is it going to rain?	_____	Vai chover?
		vy shoover?

abafado muggy	... graus	vaga de calor
aguaceiro shower	abaixo/acima de	heatwave
ameno mild	zero ...degrees	vento wind
bom tempo fine	above/below zero	vento fraco/
céu limpo clear	húmido damp	moderado/forte
céu pouco/muito	nebuloso cloudy	light/moderate/
nublado light/heavy	neve snow	strong wind
clouds	nevoeiro fog	ventoso windy
(cheio de) sol sunny	nublado overcast	
chuva rain	quente hot	
chuvisco drizzle	quentíssimo	
chuvoso wet	scorching hot	
ciclone hurricane	rajadas de vento	
fresco cool	squalls	
frio cold	ruim bleak	
gelo ice	tempestuoso stormy	
geada frost	trovoada	
granizo hail	thunderstorm	

Is there going to be a __ storm?	Vamos ter uma tempestade? *varmoosh ter ooma tempeshtard?*
Is it going to snow? ____	Vai nevar? *vy nevvar?*
Is it going to freeze? ___	Vai haver nevoeiro? *vy aver nevvooayroo?*
Is the thaw setting in? __	Vai fazer trovoada? *vy fazzair troovooarda?*
Is it going to be foggy? _	O tempo vai mudar? *oo tempoo vy moodar?*
It's cooling down _____	Vai arrefecer? *vy arryfessair*
What's the weather ____ going to be like today/ tomorrow?	Que tempo vamos ter hoje/amanhã? *kuh tempoo varmoosh tair oarje/ahmanyar?*

1.6 Here, there...

See also 5.1 Asking for directions

here/there	aqui/ali
	akee/alee
somewhere/nowhere	em algum/nenhum lugar
	aim algoom/nenewm loogar
everywhere	em todo o lado
	aim tohdoo oo lardoo
far away/nearby	longe/perto
	lonj/peartoo
right/left	para a direita/esquerda
	parra uh dirrayta/eshkerda
right/left of	à direita/esquerda de
	ah dirrayta/eshkerda duh
straight ahead	em frente
	aim frent
via	por
	poor
in	em
	aim
on	sobre
	sohbre
under	debaixo de
	debyshoo duh
against	contra
	contrah
opposite	em frente
	aim frent
next to	ao lado de
	ow lardoo duh
near	perto
	pairto
in front of	em frente de
	aim frent duh

in the centre	_____	no centro
		noo sentroo
forward	_____	para diante
		parra deeant
downward	_____	para baixo
		parra byshoo
upward	_____	para cima
		parra seema
inward	_____	para dentro
		parra dentroo
outward	_____	para fora
		parra foura
backward	_____	para trás
		parra traj
at the front	_____	à frente
		ah frent
at the back	_____	atrás
		atraj
in the north	_____	no norte
		noo nort
to the south	_____	para o sul
		para oo sool
from the west	_____	de oeste/do oeste
		di esht/doo esti
from the east	_____	de leste/do leste
		duh lesht/doo lesti
to...from	_____	a...de
		ah...duh

1.7 What does that sign say?

See also 5.4 Traffic signs

aberto/fechado
open/closed

água não potável
not drinking water

alta tensão high
voltage

aluga-se for hire

avariado/não
funciona out of
order

caixa pay here

completo full

cuidado com o cão
beware of the dog

cuidado com o
degrau mind the
step

é favor não
incomodar do not
disturb

elevador lift

empurre/puxe
push/pull

escada steps

entrada entrance

entrada livre/grátis
entry free

escada de incêndio
fire escape

escada rolante
escalator

homens gents/
gentlemen

horário opening
hours

informações
information

lavabos toilets

liquidação clearance

liquidação total
closing-down sale

não mexer do not
touch

passagem/entrada
proibida no entry

perigo danger

perigo de incêndio
fire hazard

posto de primeiros
socorros first aid

primeiro andar first
floor

proibida a entrada
de animais no pets
allowed

proibido fazer
fogueira no open
fires

proibido fotografar
no photographs

proibido fumar no
smoking

proibido pisar a
relva keep off the
grass

propriedade privada
private (property)

recepção reception

reservado reserved

saída exit

saída de emergência
emergency exit

saldos sale

senhoras ladies

sinal de alarme
alarm signal

tinta fresca wet paint

vende-se for sale

1.8 Telephone alphabet

a	_ah_	América	_amereeka_		
b	_bay_	Bernardo	_bairnardoo_		
c	_say_	Colónia	_colonnia_		
d	_day_	Dinamarca	_deenamarca_		
e	_eh_	Espanha	_eshpanya_		
f	_ef_	França	_fransa_		
g	_jey_	Grécia	_gressia_		
h	_gar_	Holanda	_ollanda_		
i	_ee_	Irlanda	_earlanda_		
j	_jotta_	Japão	_japown_		
k	_kappa_	Kremlim	_kremleen_		
l	_el_	Londres	_londresh_		
m	_me_	Madrid	_madree_		
n	_ene_	Nápoles	_napolesh_		
o	_oh_	Oslo	_ojloo_		
p	_peh_	Portugal	_poortoogarl_		
q	_q_	Quilo	_keeloo_		
r	_err_	Rússia	_roossia_		
s	_ess_	Suécia	_swessia_		
t	_tay_	Turquia	_toorkeea_		
u	_u_	Uruguai	_ooroogwy_		
v	_vay_	Vitória	_veetoria_		
w	_vay_	Washington	_vasheengton_		
x	_sheej_	Xangai	_shangai_		
y	_ípsilon_				
z	_zey_	Zurique	_zooreek_		

1.9 Personal details

surname_____	apelido *apelleedoo*
christian name(s) _____	nome *nom*
initials _____	iniciais *iniciaish*
address (street/number)	morada (rua/número) *moorada (rua/noomeroo)*
post code/town _____	código postal *coddigoo pooshtal*
sex (male/female)_____	sexo (masculino/feminino) *sexoo (mashculeenoo/femineenoo)*
nationality _____	nacionalidade *nasseeonalidad*
date of birth_____	data de nascimento *data duh nashsimentoo*
place of birth_____	local de nascimento *local duh nashsimentoo*
occupation _____	profissão *proofissow*
married/single/divorced	casado/solteiro/divorciado *cazadoo/solltayroo/divorciadoo*
widowed _____	viúva/viúvo *vioova/vioovoo*
(number of) children____	(número de) filhos *noomeroo duh feelyoosh*
identity card/passport/ _ driving licence number	número de bilhete de identidade/ passaporte/carta de condução *noomeroo duh beelyet duh eedentidad/* *passaport/carta duh condusow*
place and date of _____ issue	local e data de emissão *loocal ee data duh emissow*

2 Courtesies

● **It is usual in Portugal** to shake hands on meeting and parting company. Female friends and relatives may kiss each other on both cheeks when meeting and parting company. With men this varies according to the region.

2.1 Greetings

Hello, Mr Smith_____	Olá, senhor Smith/Olá, Seu Smith
	olah,senyor Smitzh/olah sayoo Smith
Hello, Mrs Jones _____	Olá, Senhora Jones
	olah, senyora Jones
Hello, Peter _____	Olá, Peter
	olah, Peter
Hi, Helen _____	Viva, Helen
	viva, Helen
Good morning, madam_	Bom dia, minha senhora
	bom deeah, meenya senyora
Good afternoon, sir ____	Boa tarde, senhor
	Boa tard, senyor
Good evening _____	boa noite
	boa noyt
Good day_____	Bom dia
	bom deeah
How are you? _____	Como está?
	comoo eshtah?
Fine, thank you, _____ and you?	Bem obrigado, e o senhor?
	baim obrigahdoo, ee oo senyor?
Very well_____	Óptimo
	otimoo
Not very well _____	Mais ou menos
	maiz oh mennush
Not too bad_____	Vai se andando
	vysuh andandoo
I'd better be going _____	Vou andando
	vo andandoo

I have to be going.____ Someone's waiting for me	Tenho de ir. Estão à minha espera *tenyo duh ear. eshtau uh meenya eshperah*
Goodbye _____	Tchau! *chau*
See you soon _____	Adeus! *adayoosh!*
See you later_____	Até logo! *atay loggoo!*
See you in a little while _	Até breve! *atay brev!*
Sleep well _____	Durma bem *dourma baim*
Goodnight _____	Boa noite *boa noyt*
All the best _____	Que tudo lhe corra bem *kuh toodoo lher courrah baim*
Have fun _____	Divírta-se *deeverts suh*
Good luck _____	Muita sorte/Boa sorte *muinta sort*
Have a nice holiday ____	Boas férias *boash ferriash*
Have a good trip _____	Boa viagem *boa viarjaim*
Thank you, you too ____	Obrigado, igualmente *obbrigahdoo, eeguarlment*
Say hello to...for me ___	Dê cumprimentos a... *day coomprimentoosh ah...*

2.2 How to ask a question

Who? _____	Quem? *kaim?* Quem é?
Who's that? _____	*kaim eh?*

What? _____	O quê? *oo kay?*
What's there to _____ see here?	O que é que se pode visitar aqui? *oo kee eh kuh suh pod veesitar akee?*
What kind of hotel _____ is this?	Que tipo de hotel é este? *kuh teepoo di ohtel eh esht?*
Where? _____	Onde? *ond?*
Where's the toilet? _____	Onde são os lavabos? *ond sow oosh lavarboosh?*
Where are you going? __	Para onde vai? *parra ond vy?*
Where are you from? ___	De onde é? *di ond eh?*
How? _____	Como? *commoo?*
How far is that? _____	A que distância fica? *ah kay dishtancia feeka?*
How long does _____ that take?	Quanto tempo dura? *cuarntoo tempoo doura?*
How long is the trip? ___	Quanto tempo dura a viagem? *cuarntoo tempoo doura ah veeargaim?*
How much? _____	Quanto? *cuarntoo?*
How much is this? _____	Quanto custa isto? *cuarntoo cooshter eeshtoo?*
What time is it? _____	Que horas são? *kay orash sow?*
Which? _____	Qual? Quais? *quarl? cwysh?*
Which glass is mine? __	Qual é o meu copo? *quarl eh oo mayoo coppoo?*
When? _____	Quando? *cwarndoo?*
When are you leaving? _	Quando é que parte? *cwarndoo eh kuh part?*

Why? _____	Porquê?
	poorkay?
Could you...me?_____	Poderia...me?
	pooderia...muh?
Could you help me, ____ please?	Poderia ajudar-me se faz favor?
	pooderia ajoodar muh suh faj favor?
Could you point that ___ out to me?	Poderia indicar-mo?
	pooderia eendi-eecar moo?
Could you come_____ with me, please?	Poderia vir comigo, se faz favor?
	pooderia veer comeego, suh faj favor?
Could you reserve some tickets for me, please?	Poderia reservar-me bilhetes?
	pooderia resairvar muh beelyettsh?
Do you know _____ whether...?	Por acaso, sabe se...?
	por acarzoo, sab si...?
Do you have...? _____	Tem...?
	tame...?
Do you know another __ hotel, please?	Conhece outro hotel?
	koonyes ohtroo ohtel?
Could you give me...? __	Podia dar-me...?
	poodeeah dar muh...?
Do you have a _____ vegetarian dish, please?	Tem por acaso um prato sem carne?
	tame poor acasoo oom prartoo same carn?
I'd like... _____	Eu queria...
	ew kereeah...
I'd like a kilo of apples, _ please.	Eu queria um quilo de maçãs
	ew kereeah oom keeloo duh massangsh
Can I...? _____	Posso...?
	possoo...?
Can I take this? _____	Posso levar isto?
	possoo levvar eeshtoo?
Can I smoke here?_____	Posso fumar aqui?
	possoo foomar akee?
Could I ask you _____ something?	Posso fazer-lhe uma pergunta?
	possoo fazzair lhuh ooma pairgoontah?

2.3 How to reply

Yes, of course _____	Sim, claro *see, claroo*
No, I'm sorry _____	Não, desculpe *now, deshcoolp*
Yes, what can I do _____ for you?	Em que posso ser-lhe útil? *aim kuh possoo sair lheh ooteel?*
Just a moment, please _	Um momento, se faz favor *oom moomentoo, suh fash favvor*
No, I don't have _____ time now	Não, agora não tenho tempo *now, agorah now tenyoo tempoo*
No, that's impossible___	Não, isso é impossível *now, eessoo eh imposseevel*
I think so _____	Creio que sim *crayoo kuh see*
I agree _____	Eu também penso que sim *eyoo tambaim pensoo kuh see*
I hope so too_____	Também o espero *tambaim oo eshpearoo*
No, not at all _____	Não, de modo nenhum *now, duh mohdoo nenyoom*
No, no one_____	Não, ninguém *now, ningame*
No, nothing _____	Não, nada *now, narda*
That's (not) right _____	Isso está certo (isso está errado) *eesoo eshtah sairtoo (eesoo eshtah errardoo)*
I (don't) agree _____	(Não) estou de acordo/Não concordo consigo *(now) eshtoe di acordoo/now concordoo conseegoo*
All right_____	Está certo *eshtah sairtoo*

Okay _____	De acordo
	di acordoo
Perhaps _____	Talvez
	talvayj
I don't know _____	Não sei
	now say

2.4 Thank you

Thank you _____	Obrigado/muito obrigado
	obbrigahdoo/mweentoo obbrigahdoo
You're welcome _____	De nada/foi um prazer
	duh narda/foy oom prahzair
Thank you very much __	Muitíssimo obrigado
	mweenteessimoo obbrigahdoo
Very kind of you _____	Muito amável da sua parte
	mweentoo amarvel da suah part
I enjoyed it very much__	Foi um verdadeiro prazer
	foy oom verdadayroo prahzair
Thank you for your_____ trouble	Agradeço-lhe o incómodo
	agraddaysoo lhyer oo eencomodoo
You shouldn't have ____	Não precisava se incomodar
	now preceesarva si eencomoodar
That's all right _____	Não tem de que
	now taim duh kay

2.5 Sorry

Sorry! _____	Perdão
	perdow
Excuse me_____	Com licença
	com leesensa

I'm sorry! _____	Desculpe!
	deshcoolp!
I'm sorry, I didn't _____ know...	Desculpe, eu não sabia que ...
	deshcoolp, eyoo now sabeeah kuh...
I do apologise_____	Desculpe-me
	deshcoolp muh
I'm sorry_____	Lamento
	lamentoo
I didn't do it on purpose, it was an accident	Não fiz de propósito, foi sem querer
	now feej duh propozeetoo, foy same kerrair
That's all right _____	Não faz mal
	now faj mal
Never mind _____	Deixe lá
	daysh la
It could've happened __ to anyone	Pode acontecer com toda a gente
	pod acontessair com toeda ah jent

2.6 What do you think?

What do you think? _____	O que acha?
	oo keh asha?
What do you prefer? ___	O que prefere?
	oo keh prefair?
Don't you like dancing?	Não gosta de dançar?
	now goshta duh dansar?
I don't mind_____	É me indiferente/Tanto faz
	eh muh eendeeferent/tantoo faj
Well done! _____	Muito bem!
	mueentoo baim!
Not bad!_____	Não está mal!
	now eshtah mal!
Great! _____	Optimo!
	ottimoo!
Wonderful! _____	Que delícia!
	kay delleecia!

English	Portuguese
It's really nice here! ____	Que bem que se está aqui!
	kay baim kuh si eshtah akee!
How nice!_____	Que giro/bonito!
	kay geeroo/ booneetoo!
How nice for you!_____	Que bom para si!
	kay bom parra see!
I'm (not) very happy____ with...	(Não) estou muito contente com...
	(now) eshtoe mweentoo content com...
I'm glad..._____	Alegra-me que ...
	allegra muh kuh...
I'm having a great time _	Divirto-me muito
	deeveertoo muh mweentoo
I'm looking forward to _ it	Aguardo com muito prazer ...
	agwardoo com mweentoo prazair...
I hope it'll work out ____	Espero que dê resultado
	eshpairoo kuh day resultardoo
That's ridiculous! _____	Que ridículo!
	kay reedeecooloo!
That's terrible!_____	Que terrível!
	kay tereevel!
What a pity!_____	Que pena! *kay pena!*
That's filthy!_____	Que sujo!
	kay soojoo!
What a load of _____ rubbish!	Que disparate!
	kay deeshparatt!
I don't like... _____	Não gosto de ...
	now goshtoo duh
I'm bored to death_____	Aborreço-me terrìvelmente
	aboressoo muh terreevelment
I've had enough _____	Estou farto/farta
	eshtoe fartoo/farta
This is no good_____	Assim não pode ser
	assee now pod sair
I was expecting _____ something completely different	Esperava outra coisa completamente diferente
	eshperarvah ohtra coyza completament deeferent

3

Conversation

3.1 I beg your pardon?

I don't speak any/ _____	Não falo/falo um pouco
I speak a little...	*now faloo/faloo oom poecoo*
I'm English_____	Sou inglês/inglesa
	so inglej/ingleza
I'm Scottish_____	Sou escocês/escocesa
	so eshcossayj/eshcossayza
I'm Irish _____	Sou irlandês/irlandesa
	so earlandayj/earlandayza
I'm Welsh_____	Sou galês/sou galesa
	so gallayj/so gallayza
Do you speak _____	Fala inglês/francês/alemão?
English/French/	*fala inglej/fransayj/allaymau?*
German?	
Is there anyone who ___	Há alguém que fale...?
speaks...?	*ah algaim kuh fal...?*
I beg your pardon? ____	O que é que diz?
	oo kay eh kuh deej?
I (don't) understand ____	(Não) compreendo
	(now) comprayendoo
Do you understand ____	Compreende-me?
me?	*comprend muh?*
Could you repeat that, _	Podia repetir se faz favor?
please?	*poodeer repeteer suh faj favvor?*
Could you speak more _	Podia falar mais devagar?
slowly, please?	*poodeer falar mysh de-vaggar?*
What does that word___	O que significa aquilo/aquela palavra?
mean?	*oo kuh signifeeka akeeloo/akella pallavra?*
Is that similar to/the____	É (quase) a mesma coisa que...?
same as...?	*eh (quaz) ah mejma coyza kuh...?*
Could you write that ___	Podia escrever?
down for me, please?	*poodeer eshcrevair?*
Could you spell that ___	Podia soletrar?
for me, please?	*poodeer soolittrar?*

(See 1.8 Telephone alphabet)

Could you point that ___ out in this phrase book, please?	Podia indicar aqui no guia? *poodeer indeecar akee noo gueea?*
One moment, please, ___ I have to look it up	Um momento, tenho de procurar *oom moomentoo tenyoo duh procurar*
I can't find the _____ word/the sentence	Não encontro a palavra/a frase *now encontroo ah palarvra/ah frarz*
How do you say _____ that in...?	Como é que se diz em ...? *cohmoo eh kuh suh deej aim...?*
How do you _____ pronounce that?	Como é que se pronuncia? *cohmoo eh kuh suh proonoonsia?*

3.2 Introductions

May I introduce _____ myself?	Posso apresentar-me? *possoo apprezentar muh?*
My name's... _____	Chamo-me... *shamoo muh...*
I'm... _____	Sou... *so...*
What's your name? ___	Como se chama? *commoo suh shamma?*
May I introduce...? ____	Apresento lhe... *aprezentoo lhya...*
– my wife/ daughter/ ___ mother/girlfriend	A minha mulher/filha/mãe/amiga *uh meenya moolyer/feelya/ameega*
– my husband/son/ ___ father/boyfriend	O meu marido/filho/pai/amigo *oo mayoo mareedoo/feelyoo/ameegoo*
How do you do_____	Muito prazer em conhecê-lo *mueentoo prazair aim coonyessay loo*
Pleased to meet you ___	Muito prazer (em conhecê-lo) *mueentoo prazair aim coonyessay loo*

Where are you from? ___	Donde é?/De onde é?
	dond eh?/di ondi eh?
I'm from _____	Sou da Inglaterra/Escócia/Irlanda/Gales
England/Scotland/	*so da eenglatera/eshcossia/eerlanda/*
Ireland/Wales	*garlesh*
What city do you live ___	Em que cidade mora?
in?	*aim kay sidard mora?*
In... It's near... _____	Em... É perto de...
	aim... eh pairtoo duh
Have you been here ___	Já está cá há muito tempo?
long?	*jah eshtah cah hah mweentoo tempoo?*
A few days_____	Há uns dias
	ha unsh deeash
How long are you_____	Quanto tempo fica cá?
staying here?	*cuarntoo tempoo feeka cah?*
We're (probably) _____	Partimos (provavelmente) amanhã/daqui
leaving tomorrow/in	a duas semanas
two weeks	*partimoosh (proovarvelment)*
	armanyar/dakee ah dooash semarnash
Where are you _____	Onde está hospedado?
staying?	*ond eshtah oshpedardoo?*
In a hotel/an _____	Num hotel/apartamento
apartment	*noom ohtel/ apartarmentoo*
On a camp site_____	Num parque de campismo
	noom park duh campeejmoo
With friends/relatives ___	Em casa de uns amigos/familiares
	aim carza di uns amigoosh/familiaresh
Are you here on your ___	Está cá sozinho/com a família?
own/with your family?	*eshtah cah sozeenyoo/com ah fameelya?*
I'm on my own _____	Estou sozinho
	eshtoe sozeenyoo
I'm with my _____	Estou com a minha amiga/o meu amigo/a
partner/wife/husband	minha mulher/o meu marido
	eshtoe com ah meenya ameega/oo mayoo
	ameegoo/ah meenya mullyer/oo mayoo
	mareedoo

– with my family _____	Estou com a minha família
	eshtoe com ah meenya fameelya
– with relatives _____	Estou com familiares
	eshtoe com familiaresh
– with a friend/friends __	Estou com um amigo/uma amiga/amigos
	eshtoe com oom ameegoo/ooma ameega/
	ameegoosh
Are you married? _____	É casado/casada?
	eh cazardo/cazarda
Do you have a steady __	Tens namorado/namorada?
boyfriend/girlfriend?	*taynsh namorardoo/namorardah?*
That's none of your ____	Não tem nada com isso
business	*now taim narda com eesoo*
I'm married _____	Sou casado/casada
	so cazardo/cazarda
– single_____	Sou solteiro/solteira
	so soltayroo/soltayrah
– separated _____	Estou separado/separada
	eshtoe separardoo/separardah
– divorced _____	Estou divorciado/divorciada
	eshtoe deevorciardoo/deevorciardah
– a widow/widower ____	Sou viúva/viúvo
	so veeoova/veeoovoo
I live alone/with_____	Vivo sozinho/com um companheiro
someone	*veevoo sozzeenyoo/com oom*
	companyayroo
Do you have any _____	Tem filhos/netos?
children/grandchildren?	*taim feelyoosh/nettoosh?*
How old are you?_____	Que idade tem?
	kuh eedad taim?
How old is she/he? ____	Que idade tem ela/ele?
	kuh eedad taim ella/el?
I'm... _____	Tenho...anos
	tenyo...anoosh

She's/he's...___	Ela/ele tem...anos
	ella/el taim...anoosh
What do you do for a ___ living?	O que é que faz?
	oo kay eh kuh faj?
I work in an office___	Trabalho num escritório
	trabalyoo noom eshcritoryoo
I'm a student/ ___ I'm at school	Estudo/ando na escola
	eshtoodoo/andoo nah eshcolla
I'm unemployed ___	Estou desempregado
	eshtoe dezempregardoo
I'm retired ___	Estou reformado
	eshtoe refformardoo
I'm on a disability___ pension	Estou reformado por causa de inválidez
	eshtoe refformardoo por cowza di eenvallidesh
I'm a housewife ___	Sou dona de casa
	so donna duh carza
Do you like your job? ___	Gosta do seu trabalho?
	goshta doo sayoo trabalyoo?
Most of the time___	Às vezes sim, às vezes não
	aj vaizesh see, aj vaizesh now
I usually do, but I ___ prefer holidays	Geralmente sim, mas gosto mais de férias
	jerarlment si maj goshtoo mysh duh ferriash

3.3 Starting/ending a conversation

Could I ask you ___ something?	Posso fazer-lhe uma pergunta?
	possoo fazer lyer ooma pergoontah
Excuse me___	Desculpe
	deshcoolp
Excuse me, could you___ help me?	Desculpe, podia ajudar-me?
	deshcoolp poodeer ajoodar muh?

Yes, what's the problem?	Sim, o que é?
	see oo kee eh?
What can I do for you?	O que deseja?
	oo kuh dezayjah?
Sorry, I don't have time now	Desculpe, agora não tenho tempo
	deshcoolp agorah now tenyoo tempoo
Do you have a light?	Tem lume?
	taim loom?
May I join you?	Posso sentar-me ao seu lado?
	possoo sentar muh ow sayoo lardoo?
Could you take a picture of me/us? Press this button	Podia tirar-me/tirar-nos uma fotografia? Carregue neste botão.
	podia tirrar muh/tirrar nooz ooma fotrafffia? carreg nesht bootau
Leave me alone	Deixe-me em paz
	daysh muh aim paj
Get lost	Vá-se embora!
	vah suh emborah!
Go away or I'll scream	Se não se for embora, começo a gritar!
	suh now suh for emborah comessoo ah greetarr!

3.4 Congratulations and condolences

Happy birthday/many happy returns	Feliz aniversário!
	feleej annivaisaryoo!
Please accept my condolences	Os meus pêsames
	oosh mayoosh pezamesh
I'm very sorry for you	Sinto muito
	seentoo mueentoo

3.5 A chat about the weather

See also 1.5 The weather

It's so hot/cold today! __	Que calor/frio está hoje!
	kay calorr/freeyoo eshtah oarje!
Nice weather, isn't it? __	Que bom tempo!
	kay bom tempoo!
What a wind/storm! ____	Que vento/tempestade!
	kay ventoo/tempeshtad!
All that rain/snow! ____	Que chuva/neve!
	kay choova/nev!
All that fog! _____	Que nevoeiro!
	kay nevooayroo!
Has the weather been __	O tempo já está assim há muitos dias?
like this for long here?	*oo tempoo jah eshtah aseem ah*
	mueentoosh deeash?
Is it always this _____	Aqui está sempre tanto calor/frio?
hot/cold here?	*akee eshtah semprah tantoo calor/freeyoo?*
Is it always this _____	Aqui o tempo está sempre tão
dry/wet here?	seco/húmido?
	akee oo tempoo eshtah semprah tau
	saycoo/ oomidoo?

3.6 Hobbies

Do you have any _____	Tem algum passatempo?
hobbies?	*taim algoom passatempoo?*
I like painting/ _____	Gosto de pintar/ler/fotografar/biscates
reading/photography/	*gostoo duh peentar/lair/fotoggrafar/*
DIY	*beeshcatsh*
I like music _____	Gosto de música
	goshtoo duh moosica

I like playing the _____ guitar/piano	Gosto de tocar guitarra/piano *goshtoo duh toocar guitarra/pianoo*
I like going to the _____ movies	Gosto de ir ao cinema *goshtoo duh ir ow cinaymah*
I like travelling/_____ sport/fishing/walking	Gosto de viajar/fazer desporto/pescar/passear *goshtoo duh veeajar/fazair deshportoo/passeear*

3.7 Being the host(ess)

See also 4 Eating out

Can I offer you a _____ drink?	Posso oferecer-lhe uma bebida? *possoo offeressair lya ooma bebbeeda?*
What would you like ___ to drink?	O que é que queres beber? *oo kee eh kuh cairesh bebbair?*
Something non- _____ alcoholic, please	Preferia uma bebida não alcoólica *prefferia ooma bebbeeda now alcoohollica*
Would you like a_____ cigarette/cigar/to roll your own?	Quer um cigarro/charuto/cigarro de enrolar? *care oom cigaroo/sharootoo/cigaroo duh enroolar?*
I don't smoke _____	Não fumo *now foomoo*

3.8 Invitations

Are you doing anything_ tonight?	Vais fazer alguma coisa esta noite? *vysh fazzair algooma coyza eshta noyt?*
Do you have any plans _ for today/this afternoon/tonight?	Já tem planos para hoje/esta tarde/hoje à noite? *jah taim planoosh parra oarje/eshta tard/ oarje ah noyt?*

Would you like to go ___ out with me?	Gostaria de sair comigo? *goshtareeah duh syeer commeegoo?*
Would you like to go ___ dancing with me?	Quer dançar comigo? *care dansar commeegoo?*
Would you like to have _ lunch/dinner with me?	Quer almoçar/jantar comigo? *care almoosar/jantar commeegoo?*
Would you like to _____ come to the beach with me?	Quer ir à praia comigo? *care eer ah prya commeegoo?*
Would you like to _____ come into town with us?	Quer ir ao centro connosco? *care eer ow sentroo conoshcoo?*
Would you like to _____ come and see some friends with us?	Quer ir a casa de uns amigos connosco? *care eer ah carza di unsh ameegoosh conoshcoo?*
Shall we dance?_____	Vamos dançar? *varmoosh dansar?*
– sit at the bar? _____	Vámonos sentar no bar? *vamoo noosh sentar noo bar?*
– get something to ___ drink?	Vámos beber qualquer coisa? *varmoosh bebbair qualcair coyza?*
– go for a walk/drive? __	Vámos dar uma volta a pé/de carro? *varmoosh dar ooma vollta ah peh/duh cahroo?*
Yes, all right_____	Sim, está bem *si eshtah baim*
Good idea _____	Boa idéia *boa eedaya*
No (thank you) _____	Não (obrigado) *now obrigardoo*
Maybe later _____	Talvez logo *talvej loggoo*
I don't feel like it_____	Não me apetece *now muh aptess*
I don't have time _____	Não tenho tempo *now tenyoo tempoo*

I already have a date___	Já tenho outro encontro
	jah tenyoo ohtroo encontroo
I'm not very good at ___ dancing/volleyball/ swimming	Não sei dançar/jogar voleibol/nadar
	now say dansar/joogar volleybol/naddar

3.9 Paying a compliment

You look wonderful! ___	Estás com tão bom aspecto!
	eshtash com tau bom ashpectoo!
I like your car! _____	Que lindo carro!
	kuh leendoo cahroo!
You have beautiful hair _	Tens cabelo lindo!
	tensh cabayloo leendoo!
You're a nice boy/girl___	És um rapaz amoroso/uma rapariga amorosa
	ez oom rappaj amorozzo/ooma rappareega amorozza
What a sweet child! ___	Que criança amorosa!
	kay creeansa amorozza!
You're a wonderful_____ dancer!	Danças muito bem!
	dansash mweentoo baim!
You're a wonderful_____ cook!	Cozinhas muito bem!
	coozeenyash mweentoo baim!
You're a terrific soccer _ player!	Jogas futebol muito bem!
	joggash footboll mweentoo baim!

3.10 Chatting someone up

I like being with you____	Gosto de estar contigo
	goshtoo di eshtar conteegoo
I've missed you so ___ much	Senti muito a tua falta
	sentee mweentoo ah tooah falta

I dreamt about you ____	Sonhei contigo
	sonyay conteegoo
I think about you all ____ day	Penso o dia inteiro em ti
	pensoo oo deeah eentayroo aim tee
You have such a sweet _ smile	Tens um sorriso lindo
	taynz oom sooreesoo leendoo
You have such _____ beautiful eyes	Tens uns olhos tão lindos
	taynz oonz ollyoosh tau leendoosh
I'm in love with you ____	Estou apaixonado/a por ti
	eshtoe appaishonardoo/a por tee
I'm in love with you too_	E eu por ti
	ee ew por tee
I love you_____	Amo-te
	ammoo tuh
I love you too _____	Eu também te amo
	ew taubaim tee ammoo
I don't feel as strongly_ about you	Não sinto um grande amor por ti
	now oo seentoo oom grand amor por tee
I already have a _____ boyfriend/girlfriend	Já tenho um namorado/uma namorada
	jah tenyoo oom namorardoo/ooma namorardah
I'm not ready for that___	Ainda não cheguei a esse ponto
	ayeenda now shegay ah ess pontoo
This is going too fast___ for me	Eu preciso de mais tempo
	ew preseezoo duh mysh tempoo
Take your hands off ____ me	Não te metas comigo
	nao tuh metash commeegoo
Okay, no problem_____	Está bem, não faz mal
	estah baim now faj mal
Will you stay with me __ tonight?	Ficas esta noite comigo?
	feecash eshtah noyt commeegoo?
I'd like to go to bed ____ with you	Quero ir para a cama contigo
	keroo eer parra ah camma conteegoo
Only if we use a _____ condom	Só com um preservativo
	soh com oom preservateevoo

We have to be careful __ about AIDS	Temos de ser cautelosos com a SIDA *taymoosh de sair cowtellozush com ah seeda*
That's what they all ____ say	É o que todos dizem *eh oo kuh toedoosh deezaim*
We shouldn't take any__ risks	Não podemos correr riscos *now poodaymoosh correr reeshcush*
Do you have a _____ condom?	Tens um preservativo? *taynz oom preservateevoo?*
No? In that case we ___ won't do it	Não? Então não podemos *now? entau now poodaymoosh*

3.11 Arrangements

When will I see _____ you again?	Quando é que te volto a ver?/Quando é que vejo você de novo? *cwarndoo eh kuh tuh voltoo ah vair?*
Are you free over the___ weekend?	Tem tempo no fim-de-semana? *taim tempoo noo feem duh semarna?*
What shall we _____ arrange?	O que é que combinamos? *oo ki eh kuh combinarmoosh?*
Where shall we meet?__	Onde nos encontramos? *one nuz encontrarmoosh?*
Will you pick me/us ___ up?	Vem buscar-me/nos? *vaim booshcar muh/noosh?*
Shall I pick you up?____	Posso ir buscálo/la? *possoo eer bushcar loo/la?*
I have to be home by... _	Tenho de estar em casa às... *tenyoo di eshtar aim carza aj...*
I don't want to see_____ you anymore	Não o/a quero ver mais *now oo/ah kairoo vair mysh*

3.12 Saying goodbye

Can I take you home?__ Posso levá-lo/la para casa?
possoo levar loo/la parra carza?

Can I write/call you? ___ Posso escrever-lhe/telefonar-lhe?
possoo eshcrevair lya/teleffonar lya?

Will you write/call me? _ Escreve me/telefóna-me?
eshcrev muh/teleffona muh?

Can I have your _____ Dá me a sua morada/o seu telefone?
address/phone *dar muh ah sua morrarda/oo sayoo*
number? *telefon?*

Thanks for everything __ Obrigado por tudo
obrigardoo por toodoo

It was very nice _____ Gostei imenso
goshtay immensoo

Say hello to... _____ Cumprimentos a...
coomprimentoosh ah...

All the best _____ Desejo-te o melhor
dezayjoo tuh oo mellyor

Good luck _____ Que tudo corra bem
kuh toodoo corrah baim

When will you be _____ Quando voltas?
back? *cwarndoo volltash?*

I'll be waiting for you ___	Espero por ti *eshpairoo por tee*
I'd like to see you ___ again	Gostava de voltar a ver-te *goshtarva duh volltar ah vair tuh*
I hope we meet ___ again soon	Espero que a gente volte a se ver brevemente *eshpairoo kuh ah jent vollt ah suh vair brevment*
This is our address. ___ If you're ever in the UK...	Esta é a nossa morada. Se algum dia for à Inglaterra... *eshta eh ah nossa morardah. se algoom deeah for ah eenglaterrah...*
You'd be more than ___ welcome	É sempre bem-vindo *eh semprah baim veendoo*

4

Eating out

● **In Portugal** people usually have at least three meals:
Breakfast (*pequeno almoço*) is taken between 7.30 and 10am.
Breakfast is light and consists of *café com leite* (white coffee) and
rolls and butter (*pão com manteiga*) or toast (*torradas*).
Lunch (*almoço*) is taken between midday and 2pm. It is usually quite
a substantial meal and is never rushed. Offices and shops often
close and lunch is taken at home or in a restaurant or café. The meal
usually consists of at least two courses and is often preceded by
soup. Bread is usually available on the table.
Dinner (*jantar*) is from 8pm onwards and is similar in content to
lunch. It is usually a family meal taken at home, except at weekends
and public holidays when restaurants are the preferred venue.
Some Portuguese manage to fit in *lanche* (tea) during the afternoon
whilst most cannot last until the evening meal without a snack of
some sort. Late night supper (*ceia*) is available in some bars and
small restaurants around midnight.

4.1 On arrival

I'd like to book a table for seven o'clock, please	Posso reservar uma mesa para as sete? *possoo resairvar ooma mayza parra ash set?*
I'd like a table for two, please	Uma mesa para duas pessoas, se faz favor *ooma mayza parra dooash pessoash, suh faj favvor*
We've/we haven't booked	(Não) reservámos *(now) resairvarmoosh*
Is the restaurant open yet?	O restaurante já está aberto? *oo reshtowrant jah eshtah abertoo?*
What time does the restaurant open/close?	A que horas abre/fecha o restaurante? *ah kay orash abre/fesha oo reshtowrant?*
Can we wait for a table?	Podemos esperar por uma mesa? *poddaymoosh eshpairar por ooma mayza?*

Reservou uma mesa?	Do you have a reservation?
Em que nome?	What name, please?
Por aqui, se faz favor	This way, please
Esta mesa está reservada	This table is reserved
Dentro de uns quinze minutos uma mesa fica livre	We'll have a table free in fifteen minutes
Entretanto, importava-se de esperar (no bar)?	Would you like to wait (at the bar)?

Will we have to _____ wait long?
Temos de esperar muito tempo?
taymoosh di eshpairar mweentoo tempoo?

Is this seat taken? _____
Este lugar está livre?
esht loogar eshtah leevre

Can we sit here/there? _
Podemos sentar aqui/alí?
poodaymoosh sentar akee/alee?

Can we sit by the_____ window?
Podemos sentar junto à janela?
podaymoosh sentar joontoo ah janella?

Can we eat outside? ___
Também podemos comer lá fora?
taubaim poodaymoosh comair la foura?

Do you have another ___ chair for us?
Pode-nos trazer mais uma cadeira?
pod noosh trazair maiz uma cadairah?

Do you have a _____ highchair?
Pode-nos trazer uma cadeira de criança?
pod noosh trazer ooma cadaira de criansa?

Is there a socket for____ this bottle-warmer?
Há uma tomada para se ligar este aquecedor de biberão?
hah ooma toomarda parra suh ligar esht akessedor duh beeberow?

Could you warm up ____ this bottle/jar for me?
Poderia aquecer esta garrafa/este boião?
pooderia akessair eshta garraffa/este boyau?

Not too hot, please ____
Não muito quente, se faz favor
now mweentoo kent, suh faj favvor

Is there somewhere I ___ can change the baby's nappy?	Há aqui algum lugar onde eu possa arranjar o bébé?
	hah akee algoom loogar ond eu possa arranjar oo behbeh?
Where are the toilets? __	Onde são os lavabos?
	ond sow oosh lavarboosh?

4.2 Ordering

Waiter! _____	Senhor empregado!/Garçon!
	senyor empregardoo!/garsonn!
Madam! _____	Minha senhora!
	meenya senyora!
Sir! _____	Senhor!
	senyor!
We'd like something to _ eat/a drink	Nós gostaríamos de comer/beber alguma coisa
	noj goshtariamosh duh commair/bebbair algooma coyza
Could I have a quick ___ meal?	Poderia comer alguma coisa rapidamente?
	pooderia commair algooma coyza rappeedament?
We don't have much __ time	Temos pouco tempo
	taymoosh poecoo tempoo
We'd like to have a ____ drink first	Primeiro queríamos beber qualquer coisa
	preemayroo kerriamoosh bebbair qualcair coyza
Could we see the_____ menu/wine list, please?	Poderia dar nos a ementa/lista de vinhos?
	pooderia dar noosh ah ementa/leeshta duh veenyoosh?
Do you have a menu ___ in English?	Tem uma ementa em inglês?
	taim ooma ementa aim inglayj?

Do you have a dish ____ of the day?	Tem um prato do dia/menu turístico? *taim oom prarto do dia/menu tureeshteeco?*
We haven't made a ____ choice yet	Ainda não escolhemos *eyeenda now eshcolyemoosh*
What do you _____ recommend?	O que é que nos recomenda? *oo kee eh kuh noosh recomenda*
What are the _____ specialities of the region/the house?	Quais são as especialidades da região/da casa? *quysh sow az eshpecialidardesh duh regiau/ duh carza?*
I like strawberries/ ____ olives	Gosto de morangos/de azeitonas *goshtoo duh morangoosh/de azaytonnash*
I don't like fish/meat...__	Não gosto de peixe/de carne *now goshtoo duh paysh/duh carn/duh...*
What's this? _____	O que é isto? *oo ki eh ishtoo*
Does it have...in it? ____	Isto leva...? *ishtoo levva?*
What does it look like/ _ taste like?	Com o que é que se parece?/Tem gosto de quê? *com oo ki eh kuh suh paress?/taim gostoo duh kay?*

Desejam tomar uma bebida primeiro?	Would you like a drink first?
Já escolheram?	Have you decided?
O que querem beber?	What would you like to drink?
Bom proveito	Enjoy your meal
Querem uma sobremesa/tomar café?	Would you like a dessert/coffee?
Eu queria ainda uma aguardente, se faz favor	I'd like a brandy please

Is it a hot or a _____ cold dish?	É um prato frio ou quente?
	eh oom prartoo freeoo o kent?
Is it sweet? _____	É um prato doce?
	eh oom prartoo dose?
Is it spicy? _____	É um prato picante/com muitos temperos?
	eh oom prartoo picant/com mweentoosh temperoosh?
Do you have anything _ else, please?	Tem por acaso outra coisa?
	taim por acarzoo ohtra coyza?
I'm on a salt-free diet _	Não posso comer sal
	now possoo commair sal
I can't eat pork _____	Não posso comer carne de porco
	now possoo commair carn duh porcoo
– sugar _____	Não posso comer açúcar
	now possoo commair assoocar
– fatty foods _____	Não posso comer gorduras
	now possoo commair gordourash
– (hot) spices _____	Não posso comer coisas muito picantes
	now possoo commair coyzash mweentoo picantesh
I'll/we'll have what _____ those people are having	O mesmo que aqueles senhores, se faz favor
	oo mejmoo kuh akelesh senyoresh suh faj favvor
I'd like... _____	Para mim...
	parra me...
We're not having a _____ starter	Não queremos entrada
	now keraymoosh entrarda
The child will share _____ what we're having	O menino come alguma coisa do nosso prato
	oo meneenoo com algooma coyza doo nossoo prartoo
Could I have some _____ more bread, please?	Traga nos mais pão, se faz favor
	tragga noosh mysh pow, suh faj favvor

– a bottle of water/ wine	Traga nos uma garrafa de água/de vinho, se faz favor
	tragga nooz ooma garraffa duh agwa/duh veenyoo, suh faj favvor
– another helping of...	Traga nos mais uma dose de..., se faz favor
	tragga nooj myz ooma doz duh ..., suh faj favvor
– some salt and pepper	Poderia trazer sal e pimenta, se faz favor?
	pooderia trazair sal ee peementa suh faj favvor?
– a napkin	Poderia trazer um guardanapo?
	pooderia trazair oom gwardanarpoo?
– a spoon	Poderia trazer uma colher?
	pooderia trazair ooma coolyer?
– an ashtray	Poderia trazer um cinzeiro?
	pooderia trazair oom seenzayroo?
– some matches	Poderia trazer fósforos?
	pooderia trazair foshferoosh?
– some toothpicks	Poderia trazer palitos?
	pooderia trazair paleetoosh?
– a glass of water	Poderia trazer um copo de água?
	pooderia trazair oom coppoo d'agwa?
– a straw (for the child)	Poderia trazer uma palhinha (para o menino)?
	pooderia trazair ooma pallyeenya (parra o meneeno)?
Enjoy your meal!	Bom proveito!
	bom proovaytoo
You too!	Igualmente!
	eegwalmente
Cheers!	À sua saúde!
	ah sooah sowood
The next round's on me	A próxima rodada eu pago
	ah prossima roodarda ew pargoo

Could we have a _____ doggy bag, please?	Podemos levar o resto para o nosso cão? *podaymoosh levvar oo reshtoo parra oo nossoo cow?*
How much is this _____ dish?	Qual é o preço deste prato? *cuarl eh oo praysoo desht prartoo?*

4.3 The bill

See also 8.2 Settling the bill

Could I have the bill, ___ please?	A conta, se faz favor *ah conta suh faj favvor*
All together _____	Tudo junto *toodoo joontoo*
Everyone pays _____ separately	Cada um paga a sua parte *carda oom parga ah sooah part*
Could we have the ___ menu again, please?	Podemos ver a ementa novamente? *podaymoosh vair ah ementa novvament?*
The...is not on the bill __	O/A...não está na conta *ah/oo...now eshtah nah conta*

4.4 Complaints

It's taking a very _____ long time	Está a demorar muito tempo *eshtah ah demorar mweentoo tempoo*
We've been here an ____ hour already	Já aqui estamos há uma hora *jah akee eshtamoosh ah ooma ora*
This must be a mistake_	Isto deve ser engano *ishtoo dev sair engarnoo*
This is not what I _____ ordered	Isto não é o que pedi *ishtoo now eh oo que peddee*
I ordered... _____	Pedi um/uma ... *peddee oom/ooma...*

There's a dish missing___	Falta um prato
	falta oom prartoo
This is broken/not _____ clean	Isto está partido/sujo
	ishtoo eshtah parteedoo/soojoo
The food's cold_____	A comida está fria
	ah comeeda eshtah freea
– not fresh _____	A comida não é fresca
	ah comeeda now eh freshca
– too salty/sweet/spicy _	A comida está salgada/doce/ condimentada
	ah comeeda eshtah salgarda/doess/ condimentarda
The meat's not done ___	A carne está crua
	ah carn eshtah crooa
– overdone _____	A carne está cozida demais
	a carn eshtah coozeeda demysh
– tough_____	A carne está dura
	a carn eh reeja
– off_____	A carne está estragada
	a carn eshtah shtragarda
Could I have _____ something else instead of this?	Podia trazer me outra coisa em vez disto?
	poodia trazair muh ohtra coyza aim vej deeshtoo?
The bill/this amount is__ not right	A conta/o total não está certa(o)
	ah conta/oo tootal now eshtah sairta(oo)
We didn't have this ____	Isto não nos foi servido
	eeshtoo now nooj foi serveedoo
There's no paper in the _ toilet	Não há papel higiénico na casa de banho
	now ah papell hijenneecoo nah carza duh bahnyoo
Do you have a _____ complaints book?	Tem um livro de reclamações?
	taim oom leevroo duh reclammasoynsh?
Will you call the _____ manager, please?	Podia chamar o gerente, se faz favor?
	poodia shammar oo jerent, suh faj favvor?

4.5 Paying a compliment

That was a wonderful __ meal	Comemos muito bem *comaymoosh mweentoo baim*
The food was excellent _	A comida estava excelente *ah comeeda eshtarva eshsellent*
The...in particular was __ delicious	Principalmente o/a...estava excelente *preencipallment oo/ah...eshtarva eshcellent*

4.6 The menu

aperitivos	lista dos vinhos	queijo
appetisers	the wine list	cheese
aves	marisco	refrescos
poultry	shellfish	cold drinks
bebidas alcoólicas	pastelaria/doces	serviço incluído
alcoholic beverages	confectionery/	service included
bebidas quentes	desserts	sobremesas
hot beverages	salgados	sweets
caça	savouries	sopas
game	prato do dia	soups
cocktails	dish of the day	
cocktails	prato principal	
entradas	main course	
(quentes/frias)	pratos de	
hot/cold starters	carne	
especialidades	meat courses	
(regionais)	pratos frios	
(regional) specialities	cold dishes	
legumes	pratos quentes	
vegetables	hot dishes	

4.7 Alphabetical list of drinks and dishes

açorda/camaróes à milanesa com alho
prawns with garlic and breadcrumbs

açúcar
sugar

agua mineral sem/com gás
sparkling/still mineral water

aguardente
brandy

alcachofra
artichoke

alcaparras
capers

alface
lettuce

alho
garlic

alho francês
leek

almôndegas
meatballs

amêijoas
clams

ameixas
plums

ameixas secas
prunes

amêndoas
almonds

ananás
pineapple

anchova
anchovy

aniz
aniseed

aperitivos
aperitives

arroz
rice

assado
roast

atum
tuna

avelã
hazelnut

azeitonas
olives

bacalhão
cod (dried)

banana
banana

batatas fritas
chips

batatas
potatoes

batido de...
...milkshake

bebidas alcoólicas
alcoholic beverages

bebidas frescas/quentes
cool/hot drinks

beringela
aubergine

bica
coffee - expresso

bife
steak

bife do lombo
sirloin steak

bolachas
biscuits

bolo
bun

bolo de chocolate
chocolate bun

cabrito
kid

café (com leite)
coffee (white)

caldeirada
stew

camarões grandes
prawns

camarões
shrimps

canja
broth

caracóis
snails

caranguejo
crab

carioca	costeleta	especialidades da
coffee - weak,	cutlet	região
without milk	costeleta de	regional specialities
carne	porco	especiarias
meat	pork chop	spices
carne de porco	couve	espinafre
pork	cabbage	spinach
carne picada	couve-flor	farinha
ground beef	cauliflower	flour
castanhas	cozido	favas
chestnuts	stew	broad beans
cebola	cravinho	feijão branco/
onion	clove	encarnado/frade/
cebolinha	crepes	verde
shallot	crepes	beans: haricot/
cenouras	croquetes	kidney/green
carrots	(de carne)	fiambre
cerejas	croquettes (meat)	ham
cherries	cru	fígado
cerveja	raw	liver
beer	talheres	figo
chá	cutlery	fig
tea	dobrada	filé
chantilly	tripe	fillet steak
cream(whipped)	doce	filete
chouriço	sweet	fillet
smoked preserved	entradas	filé de vitela
sausage	starters	fillet of veal
cocktails	ervas	framboesas
cocktails	herbs	raspberries
codorniz	ervilhas	frango
quail	peas	chicken
coelho	espargos	frango no churrasco
rabbit	asparagus	barbecued chicken
cogumelos	esparguete	frito
mushrooms	spaghetti	fried

fruta (da época)
fruit (of the
  season)
frutos do mar
seafood
fumado
smoked
galão
coffee – large white
gaspacho
chilled soup (tomato
  and cucumber)
gelado
ice cream
gelo
ice
grão
chick pea
grelhado
grilled
groselhas
red currents
guisado
stew
imperial
draught beer
iogurte
yogurt
língua-de-vaca
tongue
lagosta
lobster
lagostim
crayfish
laranjas
oranges

legumes
vegetables
leite gordo/meio
  magro/magro
milk – full cream/
  semi skimmed/
  skimmed
lentilhas
lentils
licor
liqueur
limão
lemon
limonada
lemonade
linguado
sole
lista de vinho
wine list
lombo de porco
loin of pork
lombo de vaca
sirloin steak
lulas
squid
maçã
apple
mal passado
  (bife)
rare (beef)
manteiga
butter
maracujã
passion fruit
margarina
margerine

mariscos
shellfish
marmelada
jam
melão
melon
mexilhões
mussels
milho
sweetcorn
miolos
sweetbreads
morangos
strawberries
morcela
black pudding
mostarda
mustard
mousse de
  chocolate
chocolate mousse
nata
cream
nozes
nuts
omeleta
omelette
ostras
oysters
ovo quente/cozido/
  estrelado/escalofad
  o/ mexido
egg – soft/hard/fried/
  poached/scrambled
pão
bread

60

pãozinho
roll

pêra
pear

pêssego
peach

paio
smoked sausage

panqueque
pancake

pargo
sea bream

passas
raisins

pastel de nata
small custard tart

pastelaria
pastry

pato
duck

peito
breast

peixe
fish

peixe frito
(carapau)
small fried fish similar
to whitebait

peixe espada
swordfish

pepino
cucumber

perdiz
partridge

perna de borrego
leg of lamb

perú
turkey

pescada
whiting

pimenta
pepper (condiment)

pimento
green/red pepper

pizza
pizza

polvo
octopus

prato do dia
dish of the day

prato frio/quente
cold/hot course

prato principal
main course

presunto
parma ham

pudim
pudding

pudim flan
creme caramel

queijo
cheese

rabanete
radish

recheado
filled, stuffed

rissol
rissole

robalo
sea bass

rodovalho
turbot

rosbife
roast beef

sal
salt

salada
salad

salada russa
salad with
mayonnaise

salgadinhos
savoury snacks

salgado/doce
savoury/sweet

salmão
salmon

salmão fumado
smoked salmon

salmonete
red mullet

salsa
parsley

sandes
sandwich

sardinhas
sardines

seco
dry

serviço (não)
incluído
service (not) included

sobremesa
dessert

sopa
soup

sopa de cebola
onion soup

sopa de feijão
bean soup
sumo de fruta
fruit juice
sumo de
  laranja
orange juice
sumo de limão
lemon juice
tâmara
fig
tamboril
monk fish
tarte de maçã
apple tart
tomate
tomato
tomilho
thyme
torrada
toast
tosta mista
toasted cheese and
  ham sandwich
toucinho
bacon
truta
trout
truta salmoneja
salmon trout
uvas
grapes
vitela
veal
veado
venison

vinagre
vinegar
vinho branco
white wine
vinho rosé
rosé wine
vinho tinto
red wine
xerez
sherry

5.1 Asking for directions

Excuse me, could I ask you something?	Desculpe, posso-lhe fazer uma pergunta? *deshcoolp possoo lher fazair ooma pergoonta?*
I've lost my way _____	Perdi-me *perdee muh*
Is there a... _____ around here?	Conhece um...perto daqui? *coonyes oom...pairtoo dakee?*
Is this the way to...? ___	É este o caminho para...? *eh esht oo cameenyoo parra...?*
Could you tell me_____ how to get to the... (name of place) by car/on foot?	Poderia dizer-me como devo fazer para ir para...a pé/de carro? *pooderia dizair muh como dayvoo fazair parra eer parra...ah peh/duh cahroo?*
What's the quickest _____ way to...?	Como é que chego o mais depressa possível a...? *como eh kuh chaygoo oo mysh depressa posseevel ah...?*
How many kilometres __ is it to...?	Quantos quilómetros faltam ainda para chegar a...? *cuarntoosh keelometroosh faltam ayeenda parra sheggar ah...?*
Could you point it _____ out on the map?	Poderia indicar-me aqui no mapa? *pooderiah eendiccar muh akee noo mappa?*

Não sei, não conheço isto aqui	I don't know, I don't know my way around here
Está enganado	You're going the wrong way
Tem de voltar a...	You have to go back to...
Aí as placas indicam-lhe o caminho a seguir	From there on just follow the signs
Aí deve perguntar de novo	When you get there, ask again

em frente	cruzamento	passagem de nível;
straight ahead	intersection	cancelas
à esquerda	estrada	level crossing
left	street	placa indicando o
à direita	semáforo	caminho à...
right	traffic light	sign pointing to...
cortar	placa de trânsito	ponte
turn	`cruzamento com	bridge
seguir	prioridade'	seta
follow	`give way' sign	arrow
atravessar	rio	
cross	river	

5.2 Customs

● **Documents:** along with your passport you must carry your
original documents with you. These include your valid full driving
licence (together with paper counterpart if photocard licence), vehicle
registration document and motor insurance certificate. Contact your
motor insurer for advice at least a month before taking your vehicle
overseas to ensure that you are adequately covered.

You may be asked to produce your documents at any time so, to
avoid a police fine and/or confiscation of your vehicle, be sure that
they are in order and readily available for inspection. It is a legal
requirement that everyone carries photographic proof of identity at all
times.

It is compulsory to carry a warning triangle in Portugal. Reflective
jackets/waiscoats must be carried in the passenger compartment of
the vehicle, not the boot (see page 70). A fire extinguisher and first-
aid kit are recommended.

O seu passaporte, se faz favor	Your passport, please
O livrete, se faz favor	Your vehicle documents, please
O seu visto, se faz favor	Your visa, please
Para onde vai?	Where are you heading?
Quanto tempo pensa ficar?	How long are you planning to stay?
Tem alguma coisa a declarar?	Do you have anything to declare?
Pode abrir isto?	Open this, please

My children are _____ entered on this passport	Os meus filhos estão inscritos neste passaporte *oosh mayoosh feelyoosh eshtau eenshcreetoosh nest passaport*
I'm travelling through___	Estou de passagem *eshtoe duh passarjaim*
I'm going on holiday ___ to...	Vou de férias para... *voe duh ferriash parra...*
I'm on a business trip __	Estou em viagem de negócios *eshtoe aim veearjaim duh neggossioosh*
I don't know how long _ I'll be staying yet	Ainda não sei quanto tempo fico *ayeenda now say cuarntoo tempoo feecoo*
I'll be staying here for __ a weekend	Fico aqui um fim-de-semana *feecoo akee oom feem duh semarna*
– for a few days _____	Fico aqui uns dias *feecoo akee unsh deeash*
– for a week _____	Fico aqui uma semana *feecoo akee ooma semarna*
– for two weeks _____	Fico aqui duas semanas *feecoo akee dooash semarnash*
I've got nothing to _____ declare	Não tenho nada a declarar *now tenyoo narda a declarar*

I've got...with me	Trago comigo...
	trargoo comeegoo...
– ...cartons of cigarettes	Trago comigo um pacote de cigarros
	trargoo comeegoo oom pacott de sigaroosh
– ...bottles of...	Trago comigo uma garrafa de...
	trargoo comeegoo ooma garrafa duh...
– some souvenirs	Trago comigo algumas lembranças
	trargoo comeegoo algoomash lembransash
These are personal effects	Estas são coisas pessoais
	eshtash sow coyzash pessooaish
These are not new	Estas coisas não são novas
	eshtash coyzash now sow novash
Here's the receipt	Aqui está o recibo
	akee eshtah oo receeboo
This is for private use	Isto é para uso pessoal
	eeshtoo eh parra oozoo pessooarl
How much import duty do I have to pay?	Quanto tenho de pagar de direitos?
	cuarntoo tenyoo duh pagar duh diraytoosh?
Can I go now?	Posso ir agora?
	possoo eer agoora?

5.3 Luggage

Porter!	Bagageiro!/Carregador!
	bagajayroo!/carreggadoor!
Could you take this ____ luggage to...?	Podia levar esta bagagem para..., se faz favor?
	poodia levvar eshtah bagarjaim parra..., suh faj favvor?
How much do I ____ owe you?	Quanto lhe devo?
	cuarntoo lyer dayvoo?
Where can I find a ____ luggage trolley?	Onde estão os carrinhos para a bagagem?
	onde eshtau oosh careenyoosh parra ah bagarjaim?
Could you store this ____ luggage for me?	Posso colocor esta bagagem no depósito?
	possoo coloocar eshta bagarjaim noo deposittoo?
Where are the ____ luggage lockers?	Onde estão os cofres para bagagem?
	ond eshtau oosh coffresh parra bagarjaim?
I can't get the locker ____ open	Não consigo abrir este cofre
	nau conseegoo abreer esht coffre
How much is it per ____ item per day?	Quanto custa um volume por dia?
	cuarntoo cooshta oom voloom por deah?
This is not my bag/ ____ suitcase	Isto não é o meu saco/a minha mala
	eeshtoo now eh oo mayoo sarcoo/ah meenya mala
There's one item/bag/ ____ suitcase missing still	Ainda falta um volume/um saco/uma mala
	ayeenda falta oom voloom/oom sarcoo/ooma mala
My suitcase is ____ damaged	A minha mala está danificada
	ah meenya mala eshtah daneefeecarda

5.4 Traffic signs

aberto
open

animais cruzando
animals crossing

auto-estrada (com
portagem)
motorway (with tolls)

bermas baixas
low hard-shoulder

bifurcação
road fork

centro da cidade
city centre

circule pela direita
keep right

circule pela esquerda
keep left

cruzamento
perigoso
dangerous
crossroads

cuidado
caution

curva a...quilómetros
road bends in...
kilometres

curva perigosa
dangerous
bend

dê passegem
give way

desvio
diversion

devagar
slow down

espere
wait

estacionamento
parking

estacionamento
proibido
no parking

estrada em mau
estado
irregular road
surface

estrada
interrompida
no through road

estrada nacional
main road

excepto
except

fechado
closed

fim de...
end of...

fim de obras
end of
roadworks

gelo
ice on road

neve
snow

nevoeiro
fog

obras
road works

passagem de nivel
(sem guarda)
level crossing
(unmanned)

perigo
danger

portagem
toll

posto de primeiros
socorros
First Aid Post

saída
exit

sentido único
one-way street

vedado ao trânsito
road closed

veículos pesados
heavy vehicles

velocidade máxima
maximum speed

via de acesso
access only

5.5 The car

● Particular traffic regulations:
– maximum speed for cars:
   120km/h on motorways
   90km/h or 100km/h outside built-up areas
   50km/h in built-up areas
– give way: traffic on the main road has priority but at intersections of equal priority traffic from the right has priority

It is compulsory for the driver and/or passenger(s) to wear a reflective jacket/waistcoat when exiting a vehicle which is immobilised on the carriageway of all motorways and main or busy roads. Jackets must be carried in the passenger compartment of the vehicle, not the boot.

5.6 The petrol station

● **Petrol is** more expensive in Portugal than in many other countries. Portugal has a good network of motorway service stations and filling stations, most of which accept payment by credit card.

How many kilometres to the next petrol station, please?	Quantos quilómetros faltam para a próxima bomba de gasolina? *cuarntoosh keelometroosh faltam parra ah prossima bomba de gasooleena?*
I would like...litres of...,	Quero...litros de... *kairoo...leetroosh duh...*
– super petrol _____	Quero...litros de gasolina super *kairoo...leeroosh duh gazooleena super*
– leaded petrol _____	Quero...litros de gasolina normal *kairoo...leetroosh duh gazooleena normal*

– unleaded petrol _____	Quero...litros de gasolina sem chumbo *kairoo...leetroosh duh gazoleena saim shoomboo*
– diesel_____	Quero...litros de gasóleo *kairoo...leetroosh duh gazollio*
I would like...euros' _____ worth of..., please	Quero...euros de..., se faz favor *kairoo...euros duh..., suh faj favvor*
Fill her up, please_____	Encha se faz favor *ensha suh faj favvor*
Could you check...?____	Não se importava de ver...? *now se importarva duh vair...?*
– the oil level_____	Não se importava de ver o nível do óleo? *now se importarva duh vair oo neevel doo ollio?*
– the tyre pressure_____	Não se importava de ver a pressão dos pneus? *now se importarva duh vair ah pressow doosh penayoosh?*
Could you change the__ oil, please?	Podia mudar o óleo? *poodia moodar oo ollio?*
Could you clean the ___ windows/the windscreen, please?	Podia limpar os vidros/o pára-brisas? *poodia leempar oosh vidroosh/oo parra-breezash?*
Could you give the car _ a wash, please?	Podia dar uma lavagem ao carro? *poodia dar ooma lavarjaim ow cahroo?*

The parts of a car

battery	bateria	*batteria*
rear light	luz da retaguarda	*looj da rettagwarda*
rear-view mirror	espelho retrovisor	*eshpelyoo retrooveesor*
reversing light	farol de marcha atrás	*farol duh marcha atraj*
aerial	antena	*antenna*
car radio	rádio	*rahdioo*
petrol tank	depósito de gasolina	*depozitoo duh gazooleena*
sparking plugs	velas	*vellash*
fuel filter/pump	filtro/bomba de gasolina	*feeltroo/bomba duh gazooleena*
wing mirror	espelho exterior	*eshpelyoo eshterrior*
bumper	pára-choques	*para shocksh*
carburettor	carburador	*carbooradoor*
crankcase	cárter	*cartair*
cylinder	cilindro	*seeleendroo*
ignition	platinados	*platteenardoosh*
warning light	luz de controle	*l ooj duh controal*
dynamo	dínamo	*deenamoo*
accelerator	acelerador	*asselleradoor*
handbrake	travão de mão	*travow duh mau*
valve	válvula	*vallvoola*
silencer	silenciador	*seelenciadoor*
boot	mala	*marla*
headlight	farol da frente	*faroll da frent*
crank shaft	eixo da manivela	*ayshoo da manivela*
air filter	filtro do ar	*feeltroo doo ar*
fog lamp	faróis de nevoeiro	*faroysh duh nevooayroo*
engine block	motor	*mottor*

camshaft	árvore de cames	*arvora duh camesh*
oil filter/pump	filtro/bomba do óleo	*feeltroo/bomba doo ollio*
dipstick	vareta	*varetta*
pedal	pedal	*pedarl*
door	porta	*porta*
radiator	radiador	*raddiadoor*
brake disc	disco do travão	*deeshcoo doo travow*
spare wheel	roda sobresselente	*rodda sobresallent*
indicator	pisca-pisca	*peeshca-peeshca*
windscreen wiper	limpa pára-brisas	*leempa parra-breezash*
shock absorbers	pára-choques	*parra shocksh*
sunroof	janela do tejadilho	*janella doo taijadeelhoo*
spoiler	spoiler	*spoiler*
starter motor	motor de arranque	*motor di arrank*
steering column	caixa de direcção	*caisha duh deeresow*
exhaust pipe	tubo de escape	*tooboo duh eshcape*
seat belt	cinto de segurança	*seentoo duh seguransa*
fan	ventoinha	*ventooeenya*
distributor cables	cabos conductores	*carboosh condootoresh*
gear lever	alavanca das mudanças	*alavanca dash moodansash*
windscreen	pára-brisas	*parra breezash*
water pump	bomba de água	*bomba de agwa*
wheel	roda	*rodda*
hubcap	tampo de roda	*tampoo duh rodda*
piston	êmbolo	*aimboloo*

5.7 Breakdown and repairs

I'm having car trouble. Could you give me a hand?	Tenho uma avaria. Poderia ajudar-me? _tenyoo ooma avveriah. pooderia ajoodar-muh?_
I've run out of petrol	Estou sem gasolina _eshtoe saim gazoleena_
I've locked the keys in the car	Deixei as chaves dentro do carro _dayshay ash sharvesh dentroo doo cahroo_
The car/motorbike/ moped won't start	O carro/a mota/a motorizada não arranca _oo cahroo/ah motta/ah motoreezarda now aranca_
Could you contact the rescue service for me, please?	Poderia avisar o pronto socorro da ACP? _pooderia aveezar oo prontoo socoroo da ey say pay?_
Could you call a garage for me, please?	Poderia telefonar para uma oficina? _pooderia telefonar parra ooma offeeseena?_
Could you give me a lift to...?	Posso ir consigo até a...? _possoo eer conseegoo atay ah...?_
– a garage/into town?	Posso ir consigo até a uma oficina/à cidade? _possoo eer conseegoo atay ooma offiseena/ah sidarda?_
– a phone booth?	Posso ir consigo até a uma cabine telefónica? _Possoo eer conseegoo atay ooma cabeen telefonica?_
– an emergency phone?	Posso ir consigo até a um telefone de urgência? _possoo eer conseegoo atay ah oom telefon duh urgencia?_
Can we take my bicycle/moped?	Posso levar também a minha bicicleta/motorizada? _possoo levar tambaim ah meenya beeceecleta/motoreezarda?_

Não tenho peças para o seu carro/a sua bicicleta	I don't have parts for your car/bicycle
Tenho de ir buscar as peças em outro lugar	I have to get the parts from somewhere else
Tenho de encomendar as peças	I have to order the parts
Isto leva meio-dia	That'll take half a day
Isto dura um dia	That'll take a day
Isto dura uns dias	That'll take a few days
Isto dura uma semana	That'll take a week
O seu carro vai para a sucata	Your car is a write-off
Já não há nada a fazer	It can't be repaired.
O carro/a mota/a motorizada está pronto/pronta às...horas	The car/motor bike/moped/bicycle will be ready at... o'clock.

Could you tow me to___ a garage?	Poderia rebocar-me até a uma garagem? *pooderia reboocar-muh atay ooma gararjaim?*
There's probably_____ something wrong with... (See 5.5, 5.8)	Creio que há algum problema com... *crayoo kuh ha algoom prooblema com...*
Can you fix it? _____	Poderia consertar isso? *pooderia consertar eesoo?*
Could you fix my tyre? _	Poderia consertar-me o pneu? *pooderia consertar-muh oo punayoo?*
Could you change this _ wheel?	Poderia mudar esta roda? *pooderia moodar eshta rodda?*
Can you fix it so it'll____ get me to...?	Poderia arranjar isto de maneira que possa seguir até... *pooderia arranjar eeshtoo duh manayra kuh possoo segear atay...*
Which garage can _____ help me?	Que oficina poderá me ajudar? *kay offiseena poodera muh ajoodar?*

The parts of a bicycle

rear lamp	luz da retaguarda	*ooj da retagwarda*
rear wheel	pneu de trás	*penayoo duh traj*
(luggage) carrier	porta bagagem	*porta bagarjaim*
bicycle fork	caixa de esferas	*caysha di eshfairash*
bell	campainha	*campyeenya*
inner tube	câmara de ar	*camera di ar*
tyre	pneu	*penayoo*
crank	crenque	*crenk*
gear change	alavanca das velocidades	*alavanca dash velocidardesh*
wire	fio	*feeoo*
dynamo	dínamo	*deenamoo*
bicycle trailer	atrelado para bicicleta	*atrellardoo parra beeceeclayta*
frame	quadro	*cuardroo*
dress guard	protector (de vestuário)	*prootetor (duh veshtooaryoo)*
chain	corrente	*coorent*
chain guard	caixa de corrente	*caisha duh coorent*
chain lock	cadeado de corrente	*caddayardoo duh coorent*
milometer	conta quilometros	*conta keelometroosh*
child's seat	cadeira para criança	*caddayra parra criansa*
headlamp	farol	*faroll*
bulb	lâmpada	*lamperdah*
pedal	pedal	*pedarl*
pump	bomba	*bomba*
reflector	reflector	*reflettor*
break pad	bloco de travão	*blocoo duh travow*
brake cable	cabo de travão	*carboo duh travow*

ring lock	cadeado de algema	*cadeeardoo duh aljayma*
carrier straps	elásticos de porta bagagem	*lashteecoosh duh porta bagarjaim*
tachometer	velocimetro	*velossimetroo*
spoke	raio	*rayoo*
mudguard	guarda-lamas	*gwarda lamash*
handlebar	guiador	*guiadoor*
chain wheel	roda de lentes	*rodda duh lentesh*
toe clip	gancho	*ganshoo*
crank axle	eixo de pedal	*aischoo duh pedarl*
drum brake	jante	*jant*
valve	pipo de válvula	*peepoo duh valvoola*
valve tube	pipo de borracha	*peepoo duh borrasha*
gear cable	cabo de velocidades/de engrenagem	*carboo duh velossidardesh/duh engrenarjaim*
fork	forqueta	*forketta*
front wheel	roda de frente	*rodda duh frent*
seat	selim	*selleem*

	Quando o meu carro/a minha bicicleta
When will my car/ _____	fica pronto/pronta?
bicycle be ready?	*cuarndoo oo mayoo cahroo/ah meenya*
	beeseeclaytah feeca prontoo/pronta?
	Posso esperar aqui?
Can I wait for it here? __	*possoo eshpairar akee?*
	Quanto é que vai custar?
How much will it cost? _	*cuarntoo eh kuh vy cooshtar?*
	Poderia especificar a factura?
Could you itemise _____	*pooderia eshpeceefeecar ah fatoora?*
the bill?	Pode dar-me um recibo para a
Can I have a receipt ___	companhia de seguros?
for the insurance?	*pod dar muh oom receeboo parra ah*
	companyeea duh segooroosh?

5.8 The bicycle/moped

● **Cycling/riding mopeds** on the roads can be dangerous in
Portugal as riders are largely disregarded by motorists, but there are
some interesting off-road tracks (unmarked). Rented cycles are few
and far between so it is advisable for visitors to bring their own – and
a crash helmet.

5.9 Renting a vehicle

	Eu gostaria de alugar um...
I'd like to rent a... _____	*eyoo goshtaria duh aloogar oom...*
	Preciso de ter uma carta de condução
Do I need a (special) ___	especial?
licence for that?	*preseezoo duh tair ooma carta duh*
	condoosow eshpessial?
	Gostaria de alugar o...por...
I'd like to rent the... ____	*gostaria duh aloogar oo...por...*
for...	
– one day _____	Gostaria de alugar o...por um dia
	gostaria duh aloogar oo...por oom deeah
	Gostaria de alugar o...por dois dias
– two days _____	*gostaria duh aloogar oo...por doysh deeash*
	Quanto custa por dia/por semana?
How much is that per __	*cuarntoo cooshta por deeah/por semarna?*
day/week?	
	Quanto é o depósito?
How much is the _____	*cuarntoo eh oo depozeetoo?*
deposit?	
	Pode dar-me um recibo do depósito?
Could I have a receipt __	*pod dar muh oom resseeboo doo*
for the deposit?	*depozeetoo?*
	Quanto tenho a pagar por cada
	quilómetro extra?
How much is the _____	*cuarntoo tenyoo ah paggar por carda*
surcharge per	*keelometroo estra?*
kilometre?	
	A gasolina está incluída?
Does that include _____	*ah gazooleena eshtah eenclooeeda?*
petrol?	
	O seguro está incluído?
Does that include_____	*oo segooroo eshtah eenclooeeedoo?*
insurance?	
	A que horas posso passar amanhã para
What time can I pick ___	vir buscar o/a ...?
the...up tomorrow?	*ah kay orash possoo passar ahmarnyar*
	parra veer booshcar oo/a ...?

		Quando tenho de vir entregar o/a ...?
When does the...have	__	*cuarndoo tenyoo duh veer entreggar*
to be back?		*oo/a ...?*
		Onde está o depósito?
Where's the petrol	_____	*ond eshtah oo depozeetoo?*
tank?		Que tipo de combustível consome?
What sort of fuel does	__	*kuh teepoo duh combushteevel consom?*

5.10 Hitchhiking

it take?		Para onde vai?
Where are you	_____	*parra ond vy?*
heading?		Posso ir consigo?
Can I come along?	____	*possoo eer conseegoo?*
		O meu amigo/a minha amiga também
Can my boyfriend/	_____	pode ir?
girlfriend come too?		*oo mayoo ameegoo/ah meenya ameega*
		tambaim pod eer?
		Vou para...
I'm trying to get to...	__	*voe parra...*
		Fica em caminho à...?
Is that on the way	_____	*feeca aim cameenyoo ah...?*
to...?		Poderia deixar-me em...?
Could you drop me	____	*pooderia dayshar muh aim...?*
off...?		Poderia deixar-me aqui?
– here?	_____	*pooderia dayshar muh akee?*
		Poderia deixar-me quando se corta
– at the...exit?	_____	para...
		pooderia dayshar muh cuarndoo se corta
		parra...
		Poderia deixar-me no centro?
– in the centre?	_____	*pooderia dayshar muh noo centroo?*
		Poderia deixar-me na próxima rotunda?
– at the next	_____	*pooderia dayshar muh na prosseema*
roundabout?		*rotoonda?*

	Importa-se de parar aqui, se faz favor?
Could you stop here, ___	*importas duh parar akee suh faj favvor?*
please?	Gostaria de descer aqui
I'd like to get out here ___	*gostaria duh deshsair akee*
	Muito obrigado pela boleia
Thanks for the lift _____	*mueentoo obrigahdoo pella boolay*

Public transport

6.1 In general

● In addition to the rather sparse Portuguese rail network, there is a comprehensive long distance coach service with good connections between north Portugal and the Algarve and between most towns and cities. The Portuguese capital, Lisbon, is well-served by its bus network, taxis, river ferries, a small underground railway (undergoing expansion) and special lifts/funiculars for getting up and down the city's seven hills.

Announcements

O comboio para..., das 10:40 horas tem um atraso de 15 minutos	The 10:40 train to...has been delayed by 15 minutes
Na linha 5 vai chegar o comboio das 10:40 para.../de...	The train now arriving at platform 5 is the 10:40 train to.../from...
Da linha 5 vai sair o comboio das 10:40 para...	The 10:40 train to...is about to leave from platform 5
Estamos à chegar à estação...	We're now approaching... station

Where does this train go to?	Para onde vai este comboio? *parra ond vy esht comboyoo?*
Does this boat go to...?	Este barco vai para...? *esht barcoo vy parra...?*
Can I take this bus to...?	Posso tomar este autocarro para ir para...? *possoo toomar esht owtoocahroo parra eer parra...?*
Does this train stop at...?	Este comboio pára em...? *esht comboyoo para aim...?*

Is this seat taken/free/reserved?	Este lugar está ocupado/livre/reservado?
	esht loogar eshtar ocoopardoo/leevre/rezairvardoo?
I've booked...	Reservei...
	reservay...
Could you tell me where I have to get off for... ?	Pode dizer-me onde devo sair para...?
	pod deezair muh ond dayvoo sayeer parra...?
Could you let me know when we get to...?	Podia avisar-me quando chegarmos a...?
	poodia aveezar-muh cuarndoo shegarmoosh ah...?
Could you stop at the next stop, please?	Podia parar na próxima paragem, se faz favor?
	poodia parrar nah prosseema pararjaim, suh faj favvor?
Where are we now?	Onde estamos?
	ond eshtarmoosh?
Do I have to get off here?	Tenho de sair aqui?
	tenyoo duh sayeer akee
Have we already passed...?	Já passámos por...?
	jah passarmoosh por...
How long have I been asleep?	Quanto tempo é que eu dormi?
	cuarntoo tempoo eh kuh dormee?
How long does... stop here?	Quanto tempo fica...aqui parado?
	cuarntoo tempoo feeca...akee parardoo?
Can I come back on the same ticket?	Também posso voltar com este bilhete?
	tambaim possoo voltar com esht beelyet?
Can I change on this ticket?	Posso mudar com este bilhete?
	possoo moodar com est beelyet?
How long is this ticket valid for?	Quanto tempo é que este bilhete é válido?
	cuarntoo tempoo eh kuh esht beelyet eh vallydoo?

6.2 Questions to passengers

Ticket types

Primeira ou segunda classe?	First or second class?
Só ida ou ida e volta?	Single or return?
Fumadores ou não?	Smoking or non-smoking?
Janela ou coxia?	Window or aisle?
A frente ou atrás?	Front or back?
Lugar sentado ou cama?	Seat or couchette?
Em cima, no meio ou em baixo?	Top, middle or bottom?
Turística ou primeira classe?	Tourist class or business class?
Camarote ou cadeira?	Cabin or seat?
Para pessoa só ou casal?	Single or double?
Quantas pessoas viajam?	How many are travelling?

Destination

Para onde deseja ir?	Where do you wish to go?
Quando deseja partir?	When do you wish to leave?
O seu...parte às...	Your...leaves at...
Tem de fazer transbordo	You have to change trains/ coaches
Tem de sair em...	You have to get off at...
Tem de fazer escala por...	You have to travel via...
A partida é no dia...	The outward journey is on...
O regresso é no dia...	The return journey is on...
Tem de estar a bordo das...no máximo	You have to be on board by...

Inside the train, coach, ship

O seu bilhete, se faz favor	Your ticket, please
A sua marcação, se faz favor	Your reservation, please
O seu passaporte, se faz favor	Your passport, please
Não está sentado no seu lugar	You're in the wrong seat
Está sentado no...errado	You're on/in the wrong...
Este lugar está reservado	This seat is reserved
Tem de pagar uma taxa	You'll have to pay a supplement
Tem um atraso de...minutos	There is a delay of... minutes

6.3 Tickets

Where can I...?	Onde é que posso...?
	onde eh kuh possoo...?
– buy a ticket?	Onde é que posso comprar um bilhete?
	onde eh kuh possoo comprar oom beelyet?
– make a reservation?	Onde é que posso reservar um lugar?
	onde eh kuh possoo rezairvar oom loogar?
– book a flight?	Onde é que posso marcar um vôo?
	onde eh kuh possoo marcar oom voe?
Could I have a...to..., please?	Queria um...para...?
	kerria oom...para...?
– a single	Queria um bilhete só de ida para...?
	kerria oom beelyet soh duh eeda parra...?
– a return	Queria um bilhete de ida e volta para...?
	kerria oom beelyet duh eeda e volta parra...?
first class	primeira classe
	preemayra clahs
second class	segunda classe
	segoonda clahs

tourist class _____	classe turística
	clahs tooreeshteeca
business class _____	classe de negócios
	clahs duh negossyoosh
I'd like to book a _____ seat/couchette/cabin	Queria reservar um lugar/uma cama/um camarote
	kerria rezairvar oom loogar/ooma camma/ oom cammarot
I'd like to book a berth _ in the sleeping car	Queria reservar um lugar na carruagem-cama
	kerria rezairvar oom loogar na carrooarjaim camma
top/middle/bottom _____	em cima/no meio/em baixo
	aim seema/noo mayoo/aim byshoo
smoking/no smoking ___	fumadores/não fumadores
	foomadoresh/now foomadoresh
by the window _____	à janela
	ah janella
single/double _____	individual/duplo
	indeeveedual/dooploo
at the front/back _____	à frente/atrás
	ah frent/ah traj
There are...of us _____	Somos...pessoas
	somush...pessoash
a car _____	um carro
	oom cahroo
a caravan _____	uma roulotte
	ooma roolot
...bicycles _____	...bicicletas
	...beeseeclaytash
Do you also have...? ___	Também tem...?
	tambaim taim...?
– season tickets? _____	Também tem um bilhete para várias viagens?
	tambaim taim oom beelyet parra varriash veearjainsh?

– weekly tickets? _____ Também tem passe semanal?
tambaim taim pass semanal?

– monthly tickets? _____ Também tem um passe mensal?
tambaim taim oom pass mensal?

6.4 Information

Where...? _____ Onde...?
ond...?

Where's the _____ Onde são as informações?
information desk? *ond sow ash eenformasoynsh?*

Where can I find a _____ Onde está o horário das
timetable? partidas/chegadas?
*ond eshtah oo orareeoo dash
parteedash/sheggardash?*

Where's the...desk? ____ Onde é o guiché de...?
ond eh oo geeshay duh...?

Do you have a city _____ Tem uma planta da cidade com a rede
map with the bus/the dos autocarros/do metropolitano?
underground routes on *taim ooma planta dah sidarde com ah reyd
it? dooz outoocahroosh/doo
metropooleetarnoo?*

Do you have a _____ Tem um horário?
timetable? *taim oom oraryoo?*

I'd like to confirm/ _____ Queria confirmar/anular/alterar a
cancel/change my marcação/viagem para...
booking for/trip to... *kerria confeermar/anoolar/alterar ah
marcasow/veearjaim parra...*

Will I get my money_____ O dinheiro é devolvido?
back? *oo deenyayroo eh devolveedoo?*

I want to go to..._____ How do I get there? (What's the quickest way there?)	Tenho de ir para...Qual é a viagem (mais rápida) para lá? *tenyoo duh eer parra...cuarl eh ah veearjaim (mysh rappida) parra la?*
How much is a _____ single/return ticket to...?	Quanto custa um bilhete de ida/ida e volta para...? *cuarntoo cooshta oom beelyet duh eeda e volta parra...?*
Do I have to pay a ____ supplement?	Tenho de pagar suplemento? *tenyoo duh paggar sooplementoo?*
Can I interrupt my ____ journey with this ticket?	Com este bilhete, posso interromper a viagem? *com esht beelyet possoo eenterompair ah veearjaim?*
How much luggage ____ am I allowed?	Quantos quilos de bagagem posso levar? *cuarntoosh keeloosh duh bagarjaim possoo levar?*
Can I send my luggage_ in advance?	Posso enviar a minha bagagem com antecedência? *possoo enviar a meenya bagarjaim com antessidencia?*
Does this...travel _____ direct?	Este...é directo? *esht...eh deeretoo?*
Do I have to change? __ Where?	Tenho de fazer transbordo? Onde? *tenyoo duh fazair transhboordoo? ond?*
Will there be any _____ stopovers?	O avião faz escalas? *oo avvyiow faj eshcarlash?*
Does the boat call in at_ any ports on the way?	O navio pára em alguns portos? *oo naveeoo para aim algoonsh portoosh?*
Does the train/ _____ bus stop at...?	O comboio/camioneta pára em...? *oo comboyoo/camioonayta para aim...?*
Where should I get off?_	Onde é que devo sair? *ond eh kuh dayvoo syeer?*
Is there a connection____ to...?	Há ligação para...? *ah leegasow parra...?*
How long do I have to__ wait?	Quanto tempo tenho de esperar? *cuarntoo tempoo tenyoo duh eshperrar?*

When does...leave? ____	Quando é que parte...?
	cuarndoo eh kuh part...?
What time does the ____ first/next/last...leave?	A que horas é o primeiro/próximo/último...?
	ah kay orash eh oo preemayroo/prosseemoo/oolteemoo...?
How long does...take? _	Quanto tempo leva...?
	cuarntoo tempoo levva?
What time does...arrive _ in...?	A que horas chega...a...?
	ah kay orash shayga...ah...?
Where does the...to... __ leave from?	Donde parte o...para...?
	dond part oo...parra...?
Is this...to...? _____	É este...para...?
	eh esht...parra...?

6.5 Aeroplanes

● **At a Portuguese airport** (*aeroporto*), you will find the following signs:

chegadas	internacional
arrivals	international
partidas	alfândega
departures	customs
voos domésticos	
domestic flights	

6.6 Trains

● **The Portuguese rail network** is still being developed and
upgraded, but there are fast services between the main cities of
Lisbon and Oporto

6.7 Taxis

● **Metered taxis** are available in all cities and large towns and are
usually black and green. In the smaller towns, it is usual to agree a
fixed price in advance as well as to check that the meter starts the
journey at zero. A supplement is normally payable for luggage, a
journey at night and on sundays or public holidays, but Portuguese
taxis are generally cheaper than taxis in the rest of Europe.

livre	ocupado	praça de táxis
for hire	booked	taxi rank

Taxi! _____	Táxi!
	tarksy!
Could you get me a ___ taxi, please?	Podia chamar um táxi?
	poodia shammar oom tarksy?
Where can I find a taxi _ around here?	Onde é que posso apanhar um táxi, aqui perto?
	ond eh kuh possoo apanyar oom tarksy akee pairtoo?
Could you take me to..., please?	Podia levar-me para..., se faz favor?
	poodia levah muh parra..., suh faj favvor?
– this address _____	Podia levar-me para esta morada, se faz favor?
	poodia levah muh parra eshta morrarda, suh faj favvor?

– the...hotel	Podia levar-me para o hotel..., se faz favor?
	poodia levah muh parra oo ohtel..., suh faj favvor?
– the town/city centre	Podia levar-me para o centro, se faz favor?
	poodia levah muh parra oo sentroo, suh faj favvor?
– the station	Podia levar-me para a estação, se faz favor?
	poodia levah muh parra ah eshtasow, suh faj favvor?
– the airport	Podia levar-me ao aeroporto se faz favor?
	poodia levah muh ow ayroopoortoo, suh faj favvor?
How much is the trip to...?	Qual é o preço da viagem para...?
	cuarl eh oo praysoo dah veearjaim parra...?
How far is it to...?	Qual é a distância até...?
	cuarl eh ah deeshtarnsia atay...?
Could you turn on the meter, please?	Pode ligar o taxímetro, se faz favor?
	pod leegar oo tazkseemetroo, suh faj favvor?
I'm in a hurry	Estou com pressa
	eshtoe com pressa
Could you speed up/ slow down a little?	Podia guiar mais depressa/mais devagar?
	poodia guiar mysh depressa/mysh deevagar?
Could you take a different route?	Podia ir por outro caminho?
	poodia eer por ohtroo cameenyoo?
I'd like to get out here, please	Deixe-me ficar aqui, se faz favor
	daysh muh feecar akee, suh faj favvor
You have to go...here	Tem de ir aqui...
	taim duh eer akee...

You have to go straight_ on here	Tem de ir aqui em frente
	taim duh eer akee aim frent
You have to turn left ___ here	Tem de ir aqui à esquerda
	taim duh eer akee ah eshkairda
You have to turn right __ here	Tem de ir aqui à direita
	taim duh eer akee ah dirayta
This is it _____	É aqui
	eh akee
Could you wait a minute for me, please?	Podia esperar um momento?
	poodia eshperar oom moomentoo?

7 Overnight accommodation

7.1 General

● **Hotels (hotels):** these are classified according to the standard of comfort offered and range from five star de luxe to simple one star, priced accordingly. The same applies to aparthotels and motels.

Pousadas: these are extremely well-appointed state-owned hotels located either in historic buildings or areas of particular natural beauty.

Estalagens: these are usually restored buildings similar to *pousadas* but privately owned and offering a good level of accommodation.

Habitacões de Turismo: these offer short-stay accommodation in large and beautiful private residences similar to stately homes. The owners are often present and the level of comfort varies.

Pensões, *residências*, *albergarias:* these are usually less expensive and offer a lesser degree of comfort than the other forms of accommodation. They are also classified and sometimes visitors to Portugal may fare better in a highly classified *residência* or *albergaria* than in a low rated hotel.

Camping: camping away from the one hundred or so designated camp sites is not usually allowed.

Albergos da juventude: there are very few youth hostels in Portugal. There is no upper age limit. Advance booking at peak times is advisable.

Quanto tempo quer ficar?	How long do you want to stay?
Preencha esta ficha, se faz favor	Fill out this form, please
Posso ver o seu passaporte?	Could I see your passport?
Tem de pagar um depósito	I'll need a deposit
Tem de pagar adiantado	You'll have to pay in advance

My name is... I've _____ made a reservation (over the phone/by mail/by fax)	Chamo-me... Reservei um lugar/um quarto (pelo telefone/por escrito/por fax) *shammoo muh...rezervay om loogar/oom cuartoo (pelloo telefon/poor eshcreetoo/poor fax)*
How much is it per _____ night/week/month?	Qual é o preço por noite/por semana/por mês? *cuarl eh oo praysoo por noyt/por semarna/por mayge?*
We'll be staying at _____ least...nights/weeks	Ficamos pelo menos...noites/semanas *feecarmoosh pello menoosh... noytsh/semarnash*
We don't know yet_____	Ainda não sabemos precisamente *ayeenda now sabbaymoosh preseezament*
Do you allow pets _____ (cats/dogs)?	É permitido trazer animais domésticos (cães/gatos)? *eh pairmeeteedo trazair aneemysh doomeshteecoosh (caynsh/gartoosh)?*
What time does the _____ gate/door open/close?	A que horas abrem/fecham a cancela/a porta? *ah kay orash abraim/feysham ah cancella/ah porta?*
Could you get me _____ a taxi, please?	Poderia mandar vir um táxi? *pooderia mandar veer oom tacksy?*
Is there any mail_____ for me?	Há correio para mim? *ah coorayoo parra meem?*

7.2 Camping

Where's the manager? _	Onde está o responsável? *ond eshtah oo reshponsarvel?*
Are we allowed to _____ camp here?	Podemos acampar aqui? *poodaymoosh acampar akee?*

Pode escolher o seu lugar	You can pick your own site
Nós lhe indicamos um lugar	You'll be allocated a site
Este é o número do seu lugar	This is your site number
Importa-se de colar isto no seu carro?	Stick this on your car, please
Não perca este cartão	Please don't lose this card

There are...of us and __ we have...tents
Somos...pessoas e temos...tendas
somoosh...pessoash e taymoosh...tendash

Can we pick our_____ own site?
Nós próprios podemos escolher um lugar?
nosh propreeoosh poodaymoosh eshcoolyair oom loogar?

Do you have a quiet ___ spot for us?
Poderia dar-nos um lugar tranquilo?
pooderia dar noosh oom loogar trankeeloo?

Do you have any other _ pitches available?
Não tem um outro lugar livre?
now taim oom ohtroo loogar leevre?

It's too windy/sunny/ ___ shady here.
Aqui há muito vento/sol/muita sombra
akee ah mweentoo ventoo/sol/mweenta sombra

It's very crowded here__
Há muita gente
ah mweenta jent

The ground's too _____ hard/uneven
O chão aqui é muito duro/desigual
oo shau akee eh mueentoo dooroo/deseeguarl

Do you have a level ____ spot for the camper/ caravan/folding caravan?
Poderia arranjar um lugar plano para o reboque/a rulote/o trailer?
pooderia arranjar oom loogar plarnoo parra oo rabok/a roolot/oo trailer?

Could we have _____ adjoining pitches?
Podemos ficar juntos?
poodaymoosh feecar joontoosh?

Can we park the car next to the tent?	Pode-se estacionar o carro perto da tenda?
	pod suh eshtasionar oo cahroo pairtoo da tenda?
How much is it per person/tent/caravan/car?	Quanto custa por pessoa/tenda/rulote/carro?
	cuarntoo cooshta por pessoah/tenda/roolot/cahroo?
Are there any...?	Há...?
	ah...?
– hot showers?	Há duches com água quente?
	ah dooshesh com agwa kent?
– washing machines?	Há máquinas de lavar?
	ah markeenash duh lavar?
Is there a...on the site?	Há neste parque um...?
	ah nesht park oom...?
Is there a children's play area on the site?	Há neste parque um jardim infantil?
	ah nesht park oom jardeem eenfanteel?
Are there covered cooking facilities on the site?	Há neste parque um lugar coberto para cozinhar?
	ah nesht park oom loogar coobairtoo parra coozeenyar?
Can I rent a safe here?	Posso alugar um cofre?
	possoo alloogar oom cofre?
Are we allowed to barbecue here?	Pode-se fazer churrasco aqui?
	pod suh fazair choorashcoo akee?
Are there any power points?	Há tomadas de corrente eléctrica?
	ha toomardash duh corrent eeletreeca?
Is there drinking water?	Há água potável?
	ah agwa pootarvel?
When's the rubbish collected?	Quando recolhem o lixo?
	cuarndoo recolyaim oo leeshoo?
Do you sell gas bottles (butane gas/propane gas)?	Vende garrafas de gás (butagás/gás propano)?
	vende garrafash duh gaj (bootagaj/gaj prooparnoo)?

7.3 Hotel/B&B/apartment/holiday house

Do you have a _____ single/double room available?	Tem um quarto simples/de casal livre? *taim oom cuartoo seemplesh/duh cazal leevre?*
How much is it per ____ person/per room?	Qual é o preço por pessoa/por quarto? *cuarl eh oo praysoo por pessoa/por cuartoo?*
Does that include_____ breakfast/lunch/ dinner?	Já está incluido pequeno almoço/almoço/jantar? *jah eshtah eenclooeedoo peekaynoo almohsoo/almohsoo/jantar?*
Could we have two ____ adjoining rooms?	Pode arranjar dois quartos juntos? *pod arranjar doysh cuartoosh joontoosh?*
I'd like a room with/____ without toilet/bath/ shower	Queria um cuarto com/sem casa de banho/banheira/duche individual *kerria oom cuartoo com/saim carza duh barnyoo/banyayra/doosh eendeeveedual*
I'd like a room_____ (not) facing the street	Queria um cuarto (não) para o lado da rua *kerria oom cuartoo (now) parra oo lardoo da rooah*
I'd like a room with/____ without a view of the sea	Queria um cuarto com/sem vista para o mar *kerria oom cuartoo com/saim veeshta parra oo mar*

Os lavabos e o duche ficam no mesmo andar/no seu quarto	You can find the toilet and shower on the same floor/in your room
Por este lado	This way
O seu quarto é no...andar	Your room is on the...floor
O número é...	It's number is...

Camping equipment

luggage space	parte resguardo para a bagagem	*part reshgwardoo parra ah bagarjaim*
can opener	abre-latas	*abre lartash*
butane gas bottle	garrafa de gás	*garrafa duh gaj*
pannier	saco para bicicleta	*sarcoo parra beeceeclayta*
primus stove	fogão de campismo	*foogow duh campeejmoo*
groundsheet	oleado	*olliardoo*
mallet	martelo	*martelloo*
hammock	rede	*reyd*
jerry can	jerrican	*gerrican*
campfire	fogueira	*foogayra*
folding chair	cadeira dobrável	*cadayra doobrarvel*
insulated picnic box	geladeira almofadas de	*geladayra almoofardash duh*
ice pack	geladeira	*geladayra*
compass	bússola	*boosolla*
wick	camisa	*cameeza*
corkscrew	saca-rolhas	*saca rolyash*
airbed	cama inflável	*carma eenflarvel*
airbed plug	pipo	*peepoo*
pump	bomba de ar	*bomba di ar*

Is there...in the hotel?	O hotel tem... *o ohtel taim...*
Is there a lift in the hotel?	O hotel tem elevador? *oo ohtel taim eelevadoor?*
Do you have room service?	O hotel tem serviço de quarto? *oo ohtel taim serveesoo duh cuartoo?*
Could I see the room?	Posso ver o quarto? *possoo vair oo cuartoo?*
I'll take this room	Fico com este quarto *feecoo com esht cuartoo*

awning	toldo	*toldoo*
karimat	tapete	*tappett*
pan	panela	*panella*
pan handle	asa de panela	*arza duh panella*
zip	feixo	*fayshoo*
backpack	mochila	*mosheela*
guy rope	espia	*eshpeea*
sleeping bag	saco de dormir	*sarcoo duh dormeer*
storm lantern	lanterna	*lantairna*
camp bed	cama de campismo	*carma duh campeejmoo*
table	mesa	*mayza*
tent	tenda	*tenda*
tent peg	cavilha	*caveelya*
tent pole	estaca da tenda	*eshtarca da tenda*
vacuum flask	termos	*termoosh*
water bottle	cantil	*canteel*
clothes peg	mola da roupa	*molla da roepa*
clothes line	arame	*ararm*
windbreak	pára-vento	*parra ventoo*
torch	lanterna de bolso	*lantairna duh bolsoo*
pocket knife	canivete	*cannivet*

We don't like this one ___	Este não nos agrada
	esht now noos agrarda
Do you have a larger/ ___ less expensive room?	Tem um quarto maior/mais barato?
	taim oom cuartoo myor/mysh barartoo?
Could you put in a ___ cot?	Poderia pôr aqui uma cama de criança?
	pooderia poor akee ooma carma duh creeansa?
What time's breakfast? ___	A que horas servem o pequeno almoço?
	ah kay orash servaim oo peekaynoo almohsoo?

Where's the dining room?	Onde é a sala de jantar?
	ond eh a sarla duh jantar?
Can I have breakfast in my room?	Posso tomar o pequeno almoço no quarto?
	possoo toomar oo peekaynoo almohsoo noo cuartoo?
Where's the emergency exit/fire escape?	Onde fica a saída de emergência/escada de incêndio?
	ond feeca ah sayeeda duh emergensia/eshcarda duh eensendeeoo?
Where can I park my car (safely)?	Onde há um lugar (seguro) para estacionar o meu carro?
	ond ah oom loogar (segooroo) parra eshtassionar oo mayoo karoo?
The key to room..., please	A chave do quarto..., se faz favor
	a sharv doo cuartoo..., suh faj favvor
Could I put this in your safe, please?	Posso pôr isto no seu cofre?
	possoo poor eeshtoo noo sayoo cofre?
Could you wake me at...tomorrow?	Poderia acordar-me amanhã às ...?
	pooderia acordar muh armanyar ash ...?
Could you find a babysitter for me?	Poderia ajudar-me a arranjar uma pessoa para tomar conta do bébé?
	pooderiah ajoodar muh ah arranjar ooma pessoa parra toomar conta do baybay?
Can I have an extra blanket?	Arranja-me um outro cobertor, se faz favor?
	arranj muh oom ohtroo coobertor, suh faj favvor?
What days do the cleaners come in?	Em que dia fazem a limpeza?
	aim kuh deeah farzaim uh leempayza?
When are the sheets/towels/tea towels changed?	Quando é que são mudados os lençóis/as toalhas/os panos de cozinha?
	cuarndoo eh kuh sow moodardash oosh lensoysh/ash tooalyash/oosh parnoosh duh coozeenya?

7.4 Complaints

We can't sleep because of the noise	Não conseguimos dormir devido ao barulho
	now consegeemoosh doormeer deveedoo ow baroolyoo
Could you turn the____ radio down, please?	Pode pôr o rádio um pouco mais baixo?
	pod poor oo rardeeoo oom pohcoo maiz abyshoo?
We're out of toilet ____ paper	Acabou-se o papel higiénico
	acarboe suh oo papell eegenneecoo
There isn't any.../there's not enough...	Não há.../não há...suficiente
	now ah.../now ah...soofeecient
The bed linen's dirty ___	A roupa de cama está suja
	a roepa duh carma eshtah sooja
The room hasn't been__ cleaned	O quarto não foi limpo
	oo cuartoo now foy leempoo
The kitchen is not ____ clean	A cozinha não foi limpa
	a coozeenya now foy leempa
The kitchen utensils ___ are dirty	Os utensílios de cozinha estão sujos
	ooz ootenseelyoosh duh cozeenya eshtow soojoosh
The heater's not ____ working	O aquecimento não funciona
	oo akessimentoo now fooncyonna
There's no (hot)____ water/electricity	Não há água (quente)/electricidade
	now ah agwa (kent)/eeletreecidard
...is broken____	...está estragado
	...eshtah eshtragardoo
Could you have that ___ seen to?	Poderia mandar arranjar?
	pooderia mandar arranjar?
Could I have another___ room/site?	Poderia arranjar um outro quarto/lugar para a tenda?
	pooderia arranjar oom ohtroo cuartoo/loogar parra a tenda
The bed creaks terribly _	A cama faz muito barulho
	a cahma faj mweentoo baroolyoo

The bed sags _____	A cama baixa muito no meio
	a cahma bysha mweentoo no mayoo
There are bugs/insects _	Há muitos bichos/insectos
	ah mweentoosh beeshoosh/eensectoosh
This place is full _____ of mosquitos	Isto está cheio de mosquitos
	eeshtoo eshtah shayoo duh moshkeetsch
– cockroaches _____	Isto está cheio de baratas
	eeshtoo eshtah shayoo duh barattash

7.5 Departure

See also 8.2 Settling the bill

I'm leaving tomorrow. __ Could I settle my bill, please?	Saio amanhã. Posso pagar agora?
	sayoo armanyar. possoo paggar agoara?
What time should we___ vacate?	A que horas temos de deixar...?
	a kay orash taymoosh duh dayshar...?
Could I have my _____ deposit/passport back?	Pode devolver-me o depósito/o meu passaporte?
	pod devolvair muh oo deposeetoo/oo mayoo passaport?
We're in a terrible hurry_	Estamos com muita pressa
	eshtarmoosh com mueenta pressa
Could you forward _____ my mail to this address?	Poderia enviar-me o correio para esta morada?
	pooderia enviar muh oo corrayoo parra eshta morarda?
Could we leave our ____ luggage here until we leave?	Podemos deixar as malas aqui até irmos embora?
	poodaymoosh dayshar ash malash akee atay eermoosh emboora?
Thank you very much __ for your hospitality	Muito obrigado pela hospitalidade
	mweentoo obrigahdoo pella oshpeetalidade

Money matters

● **In general,** banks are open 8.30am – 3pm, Monday to Friday, but closing times may vary and smaller branches may close for lunch. The sign *câmbio* indicates that foreign currency may be exchanged and proof of identity, usually a passport, will be required. Hotels will usually change money but at less favourable rates. Portugal has a large network of cash machines outside the banks and by using a UK-issued PIN number, money changing is very quick and simple.

8.1 Banks

Where can I find a _____ bank/an exchange office around here?	Onde é que há um banco/uma casa de câmbio por aqui?
	ond eh kuh ah oom bancoo/ooma carza duh cambyoo poor akee?
Where can I cash this __ traveller's cheque/giro cheque?	Onde posso trocar este traveller cheque/cheque do correio?
	ond possoo troocar esht traveller shek/shek doo coorayoo?
Can I cash this...here? _	Posso trocar este...aqui?
	possoo troocar esht...akee?
Can I withdraw money _ on my credit card here?	Posso levantar dinheiro aqui com um cartão de crédito?
	possoo levantar deenyayroo akee com oom cartow duh credeetoo?
What's the minimum/ __ maximum amount?	Qual é o mínimo/máximo?
	cuarl eh oo meeneemoo/masseemoo?
Can I take out less_____ than that?	Também posso levantar menos?
	tambaim possoo levantar menoosh?
I've had some money __ transferred here. Has it arrived yet?	Pedi uma transferência telegráfica. Já chegou?
	pedee ooma transhferensia telegraffeeca. Jah shegoe?
These are the details____ of my bank in the UK	Estes são os dados do meu banco na Grã Bretanha
	eshtesh sow oosh dardoosh doo mayoo bancoo nah grar bretarnya

This is my bank/giro ___ number	Este é o número da minha conta bancária/no correio *esht eh oo noomeroo da meenya conta bancaria/noo coorayoo*
I'd like to change _____ some money	Eu gostarià de trocar dinheiro *eyoo goshtaria duh troocar deenyayroo*
– pounds into..._____	Eu gostarià de trocar libras esterlinas por... *eyoo goshtaria duh troocar leebrash eshterleenash por...*
– dollars into... _____	Eu gostarià de trocar dólares americanos por... *eyoo goshtaria duh troocar dollaresh amereecarnoosh por...*
What's the exchange___ rate?	Qual é o câmbio? *cuarl eh oo carmbio?*
Could you give me_____ some small change?	Podia dar-me também dinheiro trocado, por favor? *poodia dar muh tambaim deenyayroo troocardoo por favvor?*
This is not right_____	Isto está errado *eeshtoo eshtah eerardoo*

Tem de assinar aqui	You have to sign here
Tem de preencher isto	You have to fill this out
Mostra-me o seu passaporte?	Could I see your passport?
Mostra-me o seu bilhete de identidade?	Could I see some identification?
Mostra-me o seu cartão dos correios?	Could I see your girobank card?
Mostra-me o seu cartão do banco?	Could I see your bank card?

8.2 Settling the bill

Could you put it on my bill?	Pode enviar para a minha conta?
	pod enviar parra ah meenya conta?
Does this amount include service?	O serviço está incluído?
	oo sairveesoo schtah eenclooeedoo?
Can I pay by...?	Posso pagar com...?
	possoo paggar com...?
Can I pay by credit card?	Posso pagar com um cartão de crédito?
	possoo paggar com oom cartow duh craydeetoo?
Can I pay by traveller's cheque?	Posso pagar com um traveller cheque?
	possoo pagar com oom traveller shek?
Can I pay with foreign currency?	Posso pagar com moeda estrangeira?
	possoo paggar com mooayda eshtranjayra?
You've given me too much/you haven't given me enough change	Deu-me dinheiro a mais/menos
	dayoo muh deenyayroo ah mysh/menoosh
Would you like to check the bill again?	Quer verificar a conta novamente?
	care vereefeecar ah conta novvamentjee?
Could I have a receipt?	Pode dar-me um recibo/talão da caixa?
	pod dar muh oom resseeboo/talow da caisha?
I don't have enough money on me	Não tenho comigo dinheiro suficiente
	now tenyoo comeegoo deenyayroo soofeecient
This is for you	Faça favor, isto é para si
	fassa favvor eeshtoo eh parra see

Não se aceita cartões de crédito/traveller cheques/ moeda estrangeira	Credit cards/traveller's cheques/foreign currency are not accepted

Post and telephone

● **Most post offices** *(correios)* are open from 9am to 5pm from Monday to Friday and until 1pm on Saturdays. Some smaller post offices close for lunch between 12.30pm and 2.30pm. Stamps *(selos)* are also sold in tobacconists' shops *(tabacarias)* displaying the sign *CTT selos*. Portuguese postboxes are red.

9.1 Post

vales postais	selos
money orders	stamps
encomendas	
parcels	
telegramas	
telegrams	

Where's...?	Onde é...?
	ond eh...?
Where's the post office?	Onde é o correio mais perto?
	ond eh oo coorayoo mysh pairtoo?
Where's the main post office?	Onde é a agência principal do correio?
	ond eh a ajencia preenceepal doo coorayoo?
Where is the postbox?	Há aqui perto uma caixa de correio?
	ah akee pairtoo ooma caisha duh coorayoo?
Which counter is for...?	Qual é o guiché para...?
	cuarl eh oo geeshay para...?
– sending a fax?	Qual é o guiché para enviar um fax?
	cuarl eh oo geeshay parra enviar oom fax?
– changing money?	Qual é o guiché para trocar dinheiro?
	cuarl eh oo geeshay parra troocar deenyayroo?

– giro cheques? _____	Qual é o guiché para os cheques `giro'?
	cuarl eh oo geeshay parra oosh sheksh jeero?
– money orders? _____	Qual é o guiché para vale telegráfico?
	cuarl eh oo geeshay parra val telegrarfeecoo?
Poste restante _____	Posta-restante
	poshta reshtant
Is there any mail for me? _____	Há correio para mim?
	ah coorayoo parra meem.
My name's... _____	O meu nome é...
	Oo mayoo nom eh...

Stamps

What's the postage for a...to...? ____	Quanto custa um/uma...para...?
	cuarntoo cooshta oom/ooma...parra...?
Are there enough stamps on it? _____	Este valor de selos chega?
	esht valor duh seloosh shayga?
I'd like...stamps of...euros _____	Queria...selos de...euros
	kerria...seloosh duh...euros
I'd like to send this... __	Queria enviar isto...
	kerria enviar eeshtoo...
– by express _____	Queria enviar isto por expresso
	kerria enviar eeshtoo poor eshpraysoo
– by air mail_____	Queria enviar isto por correio aéreo
	kerria enviar eeshtoo por coorayoo airayoo
– by registered mail ____	Queria enviar isto registado
	kerria enviar eeshtoo regeeshtardoo

Telegram/fax

I'd like to send a_____ telegram to...	Queria enviar um telegrama para... *kerria enviar oom telegrarma parra...*
How much is it per ____ word?	Quanto custa cada palavra? *cuarntoo cooshta cadda palarvra?*
This is the text I want __ to send	Este é o texto que quero enviar *esht eh oo teshtoo kuh kerria enviar*
Shall I fill out the form__ myself?	Posso preencher eu próprio o impresso? *possoo pre-enshair eyoo propreeoo oo eempraysoo?*
Can I make photocopies/_____ send a fax here?	Posso fazer fotocópias/enviar um fax aqui? *possoo fazair fotoocopiash/enviar oom fax akee?*
How much is it _____ per page?	Quanto custa por página? *cuarntoo cooshta por parjeena?*

9.2 Telephone

See also 1.8 Telephone alphabet

● **As in most** countries, telephone calls made from hotels are expensive. Most public telephones offer a direct international service, but as only low value coins can be used, a considerable quantity must be on hand. Cardphones are available and phone cards *(cartão credifone)* can be purchased from post offices. Portugal is well-served by the global mobile telephone network (GSM) and so it is well worth taking one along. Unlike in the UK, it is perfectly in order to ring someone after 9.30pm.

Is there a phone box ___ around here?	Há aqui perto uma cabine telefónica? *ah akee pairtoo ooma cabeen telefoneeca?*
Could I use your_____ phone, please?	Posso utilizar o seu telefone, se faz favor? *possoo ooteeleezar oo sayoo telefon, suh faj favvor?*
Do you have a _____ (city/region)...phone directory?	Tem uma lista telefónica de.../da zona de...? *taim ooma leeshta telefoneeca duh.../duh zona duh...?*
Where can I get a_____ phone card?	Onde é que posso comprar um cartão credifone? *ond eh kuh possoo comprar oom cartow credifon?*
Could you tell me...? ___	Podia dizer-me...? *poodia deezair muh...?*
– the number for_____ international directory enquiries?	Podia dizer-me o número das informações internacionais? *poodia deezair muh oo noomeroo daz eenformasoynsh eenternacionysh?*
– the number of _____ room...?	Podia dizer-me o número do quarto...? *poodia deezair muh oo noomeroo doo cuartoo...?*

113

– the international access code?	Podia dizer-me o indicativo de acesso?
	poodia deezair muh oo eendeecateevoo duh assesoo?
– the country code for...?	Podia dizer-me o indicativo de...?
	poodia deezair muh oo eendeecateevoo duh...?
– the trunk code for...?	Podia dizer-me o indicativo da zona de...?
	poodia deezair muh oo eendeecateevoo da zona duh...?
– the number of...?	Podia dizer-me o número do assinante...?
	poodia deezair muh oo noomeroo doo asseenant...?
Could you check if this number's correct?	Podia verificar se este número está correcto?
	poodia vereefeecar see esht noomeroo eshtah cooretoo?

Telefone para o senhor/a senhora	There's a phone call for you
Ligue primeiro o zero	You have to dial '0' first
Aguarde um momento	One moment, please
Ninguém atende	There's no answer
O número está impedido	The line's engaged
Podia esperar?	Could you hold?
Vou ligar	Putting you through
O número não está correcto	You've got the wrong number
Ele/ela não está neste momento	He's/she's not here right now
Ele/ela volta...	He'll/she'll be back...
Está ligado ao receptor automático	This is the answering machine of...

Can I dial international direct?	Posso telefonar directamente para o estrangeiro?
	possoo telefonar deeretament parra oo eshtranjayroo?
Do I have to go _____ through the switchboard?	Tenho de pedir a chamada à telefonista?
	tenyoo de pedeer a shamarda ah telefoneeshta?
Do I have to dial '0' ___ first?	Tenho de ligar primeiro o zero?
	tenyoo de leegar preemayroo oo zayroo?
Do I have to book _____ my call?	Tenho de pedir a chamada?
	tenyoo de pedeer ah shamarda?
Could you dial this_____ number for me?	Podia ligar para este número?
	poodia leegar parra esht noomeroo?
Could you put me _____ through to.../ extension...?	Podia ligar-me com.../a extensão...?
	poodia leegar muh com.../ah eshtensow...?
I'd like to place a _____ reverse-charge call to...	Queria fazer uma chamada paga para...
	kerria fazair ooma shamarda parga parra...?
What's the charge per __ minute?	Quanto custa por minuto?
	cuarntoo cooshta poor meenootoo?
Have there been any ___ calls for me?	Alguém telefonou para mim?
	algaim telefonoe parra meem?

The conversation

Hello, this is... _____	Está? Daqui fala...
	eshtah? Dakee fala...
Who is this, please? ___	Quem fala, se faz favor?
	caim fala, suh faj favvor?
Is this...? _____	Estou a falar com...?
	eshtoe a falar com...?
I'm sorry, I've dialled ___ the wrong number	Desculpe, enganei-me no número
	deshcoolp, enganay muh noo noomeroo
I didn't understand what you said	Não compreendi o que disse
	now compreyendee oo kuh deece

I'd like to speak to...	Gostava de falar com...
	goshtarva duh falar com...
Is there anybody who speaks English?	Há alguém que fale inglês?
	ah algaim kuh fala inglaij?
Extension..., please	Extensão..., se faz favor
	eshtensow..., seh faj favvor
Could you ask him/her to call me back?	Podia pedir-lhe para me telefonar?
	poodia peddeer lya parra muh telefonar?
My name's... My number's...	O meu nome é... O meu número é...
	oo mayoo nom eh... oo meu noomeroo eh...
Could you tell him/her I called?	Podia dizer-lhe que eu telefonei?
	poodia deezair lya kuh eyoo telefonay
I'll call back tomorrow	Volto a telefonar-lhe amanhã
	voltoo ah telefonar lya armanyar

● **Opening times:** Monday to Friday from 9am to 1pm and 3 to 7pm. On Saturdays shops close at 1pm, but there is a growing trend towards staying open in the afternoons. Shopping centres *(centro comercial)* are also open on Sundays and public holidays from 9am to 1pm, with longer opening hours towards Christmas. Some small shops stay open all day on Sundays. Supermarkets *(supermercado)* stay open until at least 10pm. Chemists' *(farmácia)* opening hours are the same as those of shops and the names of late-night duty chemists are displayed in the shop window and in the newspapers.

10.1 Shopping conversations

Where can I get...? ____	Em que loja posso arranjar...?
	aim kay lohja possoo arranjar...?
When does this shop __ open?	Quando é que esta loja está aberta?
	cuarndoo eh kuh eshta lohja eshtah aberta?
Could you tell me_____ where the...department is?	Poderia dizer-me onde fica a secção de...?
	pooderia deezer muh ond feeca ah secksow duh...?
Could you help me? ___ I'm looking for...	Pode atender-me? Procuro...?
	pod atendair muh? Procooroo...?
Do you sell English/____ American newspapers?	Tem jornais ingleses?
	taim jornysh inglayzesh?
No. I'd like... _____	Não. Queria...
	now. Kerria...
I'm just looking, _____ if that's all right	Só estou a ver, obrigado
	soh eshtoe a vair, obrigahdoo
Yes, I'd also like... ____	Sim, dê-me também...
	seem, day muh tambaim...

Já está a ser atendido?   Are you being served?

loja de antiguidades	drogaria	óptica
antique shop	hardware shop	optician's
armazém	electrodomésticos	padaria
department store	electrical appliances	bakery
artigos de desporto	farmácia	pastelaria
sports shop	pharmacy/	cake shop
artigos dietéticos	dispensing	peixaria
health-food	chemist	fishmonger
artigos de segunda	feira	perfumaria
mão	fleamarket	perfumery
second-hand goods	florista	quiosque
artigos fotográficos	florist's	kiosk
camera shop	frutaria	reparação de
auto-serviço	greengrocer's	bicicletas
self-service	geladaria	bicycle repairs
cabeleireiro	ice-cream parlour	retrosaria
hairdresser	joalharia	drapers
casa de bicicletas	jewellery shop	salão de beleza
bicycle shop	lavandaria	beauty parlour
casa de	launderette/laundry	sapataria
brinquedos	leitaria	shoe shop
toy shop	dairy products shop	sapateiro
casa de móveis	limpeza a seco	cobbler
furniture shop	dry-cleaner's	supermercado
casa de vinhos	livraria	supermarket
off-licence	bookshop	tabacaria
centro comercial	loja	tobacconist's
shopping centre	shop	talho
decoração de	loja de modas	butcher's
interiores	dress shop	
interior design	loja de recordações	
delicatessen	souvenir shop	
delicatessen	mercado	
discoteca/artigos	market	
musicais	mercearia	
record shop	grocery store	

Mais alguma coisa?	Anything else?

No, thank you. That's all	Não, muito obrigado. É tudo *now mueento obrigahdoo. Eh toodoo*
Could you show me..., please?	Pode deixar-me ver..., se faz favor? *pod dayshar muh vair..., suh faj favvor?*
I'd prefer...	Eu preferia... *eyoo prefferia...*
This is not what I'm looking for	Isto não é o que eu procuro *eeshtoo now eh oo kuh eyoo procooroo*
Thank you. I'll keep looking	Muito obrigado. Vou dar mais uma volta *mweentoo obrigahdoo. voe dar maiz ooma volta*
Do you have something...?	Não tem nada mais...? *now taim narda mysh...?*
– cheaper?	Não tem nada mais barato? *now taim narda mysh barartoo?*
– smaller?	Não tem nada mais pequeno? *now taim narda mysh peekaynoo?*
– larger?	Não tem nada maior? *now taim narda myor?*
I'll take this one/these	Levo este(s)/esta(s) *levoo esht (esh)/eshta (sh)*
Does it come with instructions?	O modo de emprego está lá dentro? *oo modoo di empraygoo eshtah la dentroo?*
It's too expensive	Acho demasiado caro *achoo demaziardoo caroo*
I'll give you...	Ofereço-lhe... *oferessoo lya...*
Could you keep this for me? I'll come back for it later	Importa-se de me guardar isto? Volto já a buscar *eemporta suh duh muh gwardar eeshtoo? Voltoo jah booshcar*

Lamento, mas não temos	I'm sorry, we don't have that
Lamento, já não temos mais	I'm sorry, we're sold out
Lamento, só vamos receber isso dentro de...	I'm sorry, that won't be in until...
Pode pagar na caixa	You can pay at the cash desk
Não aceitamos cartões de crédito	We don't accept credit cards
Não aceitamos traveller cheques	We don't accept traveller's cheques
Não aceitamos moedas estrangeiras	We don't accept foreign currency

Have you got a bag? __ Tem um saco?
taim oom sarcoo?

Could you giftwrap ____ Pode embrulhar como prenda, se faz
it, please? favor?
pod embrulyar comoo prenda, suh faj favvor?

10.2 Food

I'd like a hundred _____ Eu queria cem gramas de...
grams of... *eyoo kerria saim grarmash duh ...*
– five hundred grams/ __ Eu queria meio quilo de...
half a kilo of... *eyoo kerria mayoo keeloo duh...*
– a kilo of... _____ Eu queria um quilo de...
eyoo kerria oom keeloo duh...
Could you...? _____ Importa-se de...?
eemporta suh duh...?
Could you slice it/ _____ Importa-se de cortar em fatias/bocados,
dice it, please? se faz favor?
eemporta suh duh cortar aim fateeash/boocardoosh, suh faj favvor?

Could you grate it, please?	Importa-se de o ralar, se faz favor?
	eemporta suh duh oo rallar, suh faj favvor?
Can I order it?	Posso encomendar?
	possoo aincoomendar?
I'll pick it up tomorrow/_ at...	Venho buscar amanhã/às...horas
	venyoo booshcar armanyar/ush...orash
Can you eat/drink this?_	Pode-se comer/beber?
	pod se coomair/bebbair
What's in it?	De que é feito?
	duh kee eh faytoo?

10.3 Clothing and shoes

I saw something in the _ window. Shall I point it out?	Vi uma coisa na montra. Posso lhe mostrar?
	vee ooma coyza na montra. possoo lya mooshtrar?
I'd like something to ___ go with this	Queria uma coisa para condizer com isto
	kerria ooma coyza parra condeezair com eeshtoo
Do you have shoes ____ in this same colour?	Tem sapatos nesta mesma cor?
	taim sapartoosh neshta mejma cor?
I'm a size...in the UK ___	Na Grã Bretanha o meu número é...
	na grar bretarnya oo mayoo noomeroo eh...
Can I try this on? _____	Posso experimentar?
	possoo eshprimentar?
Where's the fitting _____ room?	Onde fica o gabinete de prova?
	ond feeca oo gabeenet duh provva?
It doesn't fit	Não me serve
	now muh sairve
This is the right size____	Esta medida é boa
	eshta medeeda eh boa
It doesn't suit me _____	Não me fica bem
	now muh feeca baim

Não passar a ferro	Limpar a seco
Do not iron	Dry clean
Não centrifugar	Lavar à mão
Do not spin dry	Hand wash
Pendurar molhado	Lavar à máquina
Drip dry	Machine wash

Do you have this/_____ these in...?	Tem também isto em...
	taim tambaim eeshtoo aim...
I find the heel too _____ high/low	Acho o salto demasiado alto/baixo
	ashoo oo saltoo demaziardoo altoo/byshoo
Is this genuine leather? _	Isto é couro verdadeiro?
	eeshtoo eh cooroo verdadayroo?
I'm looking for a... _____ for a...-year-old baby/child	Procuro um...para um bébé/uma criança de...anos
	procooroo oom...parra oom baybay/ooma criansa duh...arnoosh
I'd prefer a...of..._____	Eu preferia um...de...
	eyoo prefferia oom...duh...
– silk _____	Eu preferia um...de seda
	eyoo prefferia oom...duh sayda
– cotton _____	Eu preferia um...de algodão
	eyoo prefferia oom...duh algoodow
– wool_____	Eu preferia um...de lã
	eyoo prefferia oom... duh lang
– linen_____	Eu preferia um...de linho
	eyoo prefferia oom...duh leenyoo
What temperature _____ can I wash it at?	A que temperatura é que posso lavar?
	a kay temperatoora eh kuh possoo lavar?
Will it shrink in the _____ wash?	Encolhe ao lavar?
	aincollye ow lavar?

At the cobbler's

Could you mend_____ these shoes?	Pode arranjar-me estes sapatos? *pod arranjar muh eshtash sapartoosh?*
Could you put new ____ soles/heels on these?	Poderia pôr aqui solas novas/saltos novos? *pooderia poor akee solash novash/saltoosh novoosh?*
When will they be_____ ready?	Quando estão prontos? *cuarndoo eshtow prontoosh?*
I'd like... _____	Eu queria... *eyoo kerria...*
– a tin of shoe polish____	Eu queria uma caixa de pomada *eyoo kerria ooma caisha duh poomarda*
– a pair of shoelaces ____	Eu queria um par de atacadores *eyoo kerria oom par duh attackadooresh*

10.4 Photographs and video

I'd like a film for this ____ camera, please	Eu queria um rolo para esta máquina, se faz favor *eyoo kerria oom rolloo parra eshta markina, suh faj favvor*
– a cartridge _____	Eu queria uma cassette *eyoo kerria ooma cassett*
– a slide film _____	Eu queria um rolo de diapositivos *eyoo kerria oom rolloo duh diaposeeteevoosh*
– a film cartridge _____	Eu queria um cassette para filmar *eyoo kerria oom cassett parra feelmar*
– a videotape _____	Eu queria um cassette de vídeo *eyoo kerria oom cassett duh veedyoo*

– a colour/black and ___ white film	Eu queria um rolo a cores/a preto e branco
	eyoo kerria oom rolloo ah cooresh/ah praytoo e brancoo
– a super eight film ___	Eu queria um filme super de 8mm
	eyoo kerria oom feelm soopair duh 8mm
– a 12/24/36 ___ exposures film	Eu queria um rolo de 12/24/36 fotografias
	eyoo kerria oom rolloo duh 12/24/36 fotografeeash
– a film of...ASA ___	Eu queria um rolo de ISO...
	eyoo kerria oom rolloo duh ee ess oo...
– a daylight film ___	Eu queria um rolo para luz natural
	eyoo kerria oom rollo parra looj naturarl
– a film for artificial ___ light	Eu queria um rolo para luz artificial
	eyoo kerria oom rolloo parra looj artifeeciarl

Problems

Could you load the ___ film for me?	Importa-se de colocar o rolo na máquina?
	eemporta suh duh cooloocar oo rolloo na markina?
Could you take the film ___ out for me?	Importa-se de tirar o rolo da máquina?
	eemporta suh duh teerar oo rolloo da markina?
Should I replace ___ the batteries?	Tenho de substituir as pilhas?
	tenyoo duh soobshteetweer ash peelyash?
Could you have a look ___ at my camera? It's not working	Importa-se de ver a minha máquina/câmara? Não trabalha
	eemporta suh duh vair a meenya markina/camera? Now trabalya
The...is broken ___	O...está estragado
	oo...eshtah eshtragardoo

The film's jammed _____	O rolo está preso
	oo rolloo eshtah prayzoo
The film's broken _____	O rolo está partido
	oo rolloo eshtah parteedoo
The flash isn't working _	O flash não funciona
	oo flash now foonsyona

Processing and prints

I'd like to have this film _ developed/printed	Eu queria mandar revelar/ reproduzir este rolo
	eyoo kerria mandar revelar/ reprodoozeer esht rolloo
I'd like...prints from _____ each negative	Eu queria...cópias de cada negativo
	eyoo kerria...copeeash duh cadda negateevoo
I'd like glossy/mat _____ prints	Eu queria cópias brilhantes/mates
	eyoo kerria copeeash breelyantesh/matsh
I'd like 6x9 prints _____	Eu queria cópias seis por nove
	eyoo kerria copeeash saysh poor nov
I'd like to order _____ these photos	Eu queria encomendar estas fotos
	eyoo kerria aincoomendar eshtash fotoosh
I'd like to have this_____ photo enlarged	Eu queria mandar ampliar esta foto
	eyoo kerria mandar ampliar eshta fotoo
How much is_____ processing?	Quanto custa a revelação?
	cuarntoo cooshta a revellasow?
How much is printing? _	Quanto custa a reprodução?
	cuarntoo cooshta a reprodoosow?
How much is it _____ to re-order?	Quanto custa mandar fazer mais cópias?
	cuarntoo cooshta mandar fazair mysh copeeash?
How much is an _____ enlargement?	Quanto custa uma ampliação?
	cuarntoo cooshta ooma ampleeasow
When will they _____ be ready?	Quando estão prontas?
	cuarndoo eshtow prontash?

10.5 At the hairdresser's

Do I have to make an appointment?	Tenho de marcar hora? *tenyoo duh marcar ora?*
Can I come in straight away?	Pode atender-me já? *pod atendair muh jah?*
How long will I have to wait?	Quanto tempo tenho de esperar? *quarntoo tempoo tenyoo duh eshpairar?*
I'd like a hairwash/ haircut	Eu queria lavar/cortar o meu cabelo *eyoo kerria lavar/cortar oo mayoo cabayloo*
I'd like a shampoo for oily/dry hair	Eu queria um champô para cabelo gorduroso/seco *eyoo kerria oom shampoh parra cabayloo gordooroso/saycoo*
– an anti-dandruff shampoo	Eu queria um champô contra a caspa *eyoo kerria oom shampoh contra a cashpa*
– a shampoo for permed/coloured hair	Eu queria um champô para cabelo com permanente/pintado *eyoo kerria oom shampoh parra cabayloo com permanent/peentardoo*
– a colour rinse shampoo	Eu queria um champô com cor *eyoo kerria oom shampoh com cor*
– a shampoo with conditioner	Eu queria um champô com condicionador *eyoo kerria oom shampoh com condicionardoor*
– highlights	Eu queria madeixas *eyoo kerria madayshash*
Do you have a colour chart, please?	Tem um catálogo com as cores? *taim oom cataloggoo com ash coresh?*
I want to keep it the same colour	Eu queria manter a mesma cor *eyoo kerria mantair a mejma cor*
I'd like my hair darker/lighter	Eu queria o cabelo mais escuro/claro *eyoo kerria oo cabayloo maiz eshcooroo/claroo*

I'd like/I don't want ____ hairspray	Quero (não quero) laca no meu cabelo
	cairoo (now cairoo) larca noo mayoo cabayloo
– gel ____	Quero (não quero) gel
	cairoo (now cairoo) jel
– mousse ____	Quero (não quero) mousse
	cairoo (now cairoo) mousse
I'd like a short fringe ____	Queria a franja curta
	kerria a franja coorta
Not too short at the ____ back	Atrás não queria demasiado curto
	atraj now kerria demaziardoo coortoo
Not too long here ____	Aqui não quero muito comprido
	akee now cairoo mweentoo coompreedoo
I'd like (just a few) ____ curls	Quero (não muitos) caracóis
	cairoo (now mueentoosh) carracoysh
It needs a little/ ____ a lot taken off	Corte um pouco/bastante
	cort oom poecoo/bashtant
I want a completely ____ different style	Queria um modelo totalmente diferente
	kerria oom moodeloo tootalment deeferent
I'd like it as... ____	Queria o meu cabelo como...
	kerria oo mayoo cabayloo comoo...
– that lady's ____	Queria o meu cabelo como o daquela senhora
	kerria oo may cabayloo comoo oo dakella senyora
– in this photo ____	Queria o meu cabelo como o desta foto
	kerria oo mayoo cabayloo comoo oo desta fotoo
Could you put the ____ drier up/down a bit?	Podia pôr o secador mais forte/fraco?
	poodia poor oo secadoor maish fort/frarcoo?
I'd like a facial ____	Queria uma máscara para o rosto
	kerria ooma mashcara parra oo roshtoo
– a manicure ____	Queria que me fizesse uma manicure
	kerria kuh me feezess ooma manicure
– a massage ____	Queria uma massagem
	kerria ooma massarjaim

Como deseja o cabelo cortado?	How do you want it cut?
Que modelo deseja?	What style did you have in mind?
Que cor deseja?	What colour do you want it?
Esta temperatura está boa?	Is the temperature all right for you?
Deseja alguma coisa para ler?	Would you like something to read?
Deseja beber alguma coisa?	Would you like a drink?
Está bem assim?	Is this what you had in mind?

Could you trim my fringe?	Podia aparar-me a franja?
	poodia aparar muh a franja?
– my beard?	Podia aparar-me a barba?
	poodia aparar muh a barba?
– my moustache?	Podia aparar-me o bigode?
	poodia aparar muh oo beegod?
I'd like a shave, please	A barba, se faz favor
	a barba, se faj favvor
I'd like a wet shave	Queria a barba feita com navalha
	kerria a barba fayta com navaly

11

At the Tourist Information Centre

11.1 Places of interest

Where's the Tourist Information Centre?	Onde é o posto de turismo? *ond eh oo poshtoo duh tooreeshmoo?*
Do you have a city map?	Tem uma planta da cidade? *taim ooma planta dah sidarde?*
Where is the museum?	Onde é o museu? *ond eh oo moozayoo?*
Where can I find a church?	Onde há uma igreja? *ond ah ooma eegrayja?*
Could you give me some information about...?	Podia dar-me alguma informação sobre...? *poodia dar muh algooma eenformasow sobre...?*
How much do we have to pay you?	Quanto é que temos de lhe pagar? *cuarntoo eh kuh taymoosh duh lya pagar?*
What are the main places of interest?	Quais são as atrações mais importantes? *quysh sow ash atrasoynsh maiz eemportantesh?*
Could you point them out on the map?	Podia indicá-las no mapa? *poodia eendeecar lash noo marpa?*
What do you recommend?	O que é que nos aconselha? *oo kuh eh kuh nooz aconselya?*
We'll be here for a few hours	Ficamos aqui umas horas *feecarmoos akee oomash orash*
– a day	Ficamos aqui um dia *feecarmoos akee oom deah*

– a week _____	Ficamos aqui uma semana
	feecarmoos akee ooma semarna
We're interested in... ___	Estamos interessados em...
	eshtarmoosh eenteressardoosh aim...
Is there a scenic walk ___ around the city?	Podemos fazer um passeio turístico pela cidade?
	poodaymoosh fazair oom passayoo tooreeshteecoo pella sidarde?
How long does it take? _	Quanto tempo demora?
	cuarntoo tempoo demoora?
Where does it _____ start/end?	Onde começa/acaba?
	ond comessa/acarba?
Are there any boat _____ cruises here?	Há aqui barcos de excursão?
	ah akee barcoosh duh eshcoorsow?
Where can we board? __	Onde é que podemos embarcar?
	ond eh kuh poodaymoosh embarcar?
Are there any bus _____ tours?	Há excursões de autocarro?
	ah eshcoorsoynsh duh outoocahroo?
Where do we get on? __	Onde é que podemos entrar?
	ond eh kuh poodaymoosh entrar?
Is there a guide who ___ speaks English?	Há um guia que fale inglês?
	ah oom gueeah kuh fal eenglayj?
What trips can we take _ around the area?	Que passeios podemos dar nos arredores?
	kay passayoosh poodaymoosh dar nooz arredooresh?
Are there any_____ excursions?	Há excursões?
	ah eshcoorsoynsh?
Where do they go to? __	Para onde vão as excursões?
	parra ond vow az eshcoorsoynsh?

We'd like to go to... ___	Nós queremos ir a...
	nosh kerraymooz eer ah...
How long is the _____ excursion?	Quanto tempo demora a excursão?
	cuarntoo tempoo demoora ah eshcoorsow?
How long do we_____ stay in...?	Quanto tempo ficamos em...?
	cuarntoo tempoo feecarmoosh aim...?
Are there any guided ___ tours?	Há visitas guiadas?
	ah veezeetash gueeardash?
How much free time ___ will we have there?	Quanto tempo temos só para nós?
	cuarntoo tempoo taymoosh soh parra noj?
We want to go hiking___	Queriamos fazer uma caminhada
	kerriamoosh fazair ooma cameenyarda
Can we hire a guide? __	Podemos contratar um guia?
	poodaymoosh contratar oom gueeah?
Can I book mountain___ huts?	Posso reservar abrigos?
	possoo resairvar abreegoosh?
What time does..._____ open/close?	A que horas abre/fecha...?
	ah kay orash abre/faysha...?
What days is...open/ ___ closed?	Em que dias está aberto/fechado...?
	aim kuh deeash eshtah abairtoo/fechardoo...?
What's the admission __ price?	Quanto custa a entrada?
	cuarntoo cooshta ah entrarda?
Is there a group _____ discount?	Há desconto para grupos?
	ah deshcontoo parra groopoosh?
Is there a child _____ discount?	Há desconto para crianças?
	ah deshcontoo parra creeansash?
Is there a discount ___ for pensioners?	Há desconto para reformados?
	ah deshcontoo parra reformardoosh?

Can I take (flash) photos/can I film here?	Posso aqui fotografar (com flash)/filmar? *possoo akee fotografar (com flash)/feelmar?*
Do you have any postcards of...?	Vende postais com...? *vend pooshtysh com...?*
Do you have an English...?	Tem um/uma...em inglês? *taim oom/ooma...aim eenglayj?*
– catalogue?	Tem um catálogo em inglês? *taim oom catalogoo aim eenglayj?*
– programme?	Tem um programa em inglês? *taim oom proograrma aim eenglayj?*
– brochure?	Tem um folheto em inglês? *taim oom foolyetoo aim eenglayj?*

11.2 Going out

● **There are far fewer cinemas in Portugal** than in the UK.
Usherettes will normally expect a small tip. Most films shown are in
English with Portuguese subtitles, which is very convenient.
Sometimes the name given to the film in Portuguese is completely
different from its original. Details of theatre and cinema programmes
are to be found in the national newspapers, especially in the Friday
editions. Showings are generally much later than in the UK and
theatre performances are often subject to considerable delay.

Do you have this week's/month's entertainment guide?	Tem o jornal de espectáculos desta semana/deste mês? *taim oo jornarl di eshpetarcooloosh deshta semarna/deshta mayge?*
What's on tonight?	O que é que há para fazer esta noite? *oo kee eh kuh ah parra fazzair eshta noyt?*
We want to go to...	Queríamos ir a... *kerriamoosh eer ah...*

Which films are showing?	Que filmes estão a passar? *kuh feelmesh eshtow ah passar?*
What sort of film is it?	Que género de filme é? *kuh jenroo duh feelm eh?*
It's suitable for all ages	É para todas as idades *eh parra toedaz az eedardesh*
It's only for people above 12/16 years	É só para pessoas acima dos 12/16 anos *eh sooh parra pessowash aseema dooz 12/16 arnoosh*
It's the original version	É a versão original *eh ah versow ooreegeenarl*
It's subtitled	É com legendas *eh com lejendash*
It's dubbed	É dobrado *eh doobrardoo*
Is it a continuous showing?	São sessões contínuas? *sow sessoynsh conteenooash?*
What's on at...?	Qual é o programa do...? *quarl eh oo proogrrarma doo...?*
– the theatre?	Qual é o programa do teatro? *quarl eh oo proogrrarma doo teeartroo?*
– the concert hall?	Qual é o programa de concertos? *quarl eh oo proogrrarma duh consairtoosh?*
– the opera?	Qual é o programa da ópera? *quarl eh oo proogrrarma dah ohpairah?*
Where can I find a good disco around here?	Onde é que há uma boa discoteca aqui? *ond eh kuh ha ooma boa deeshcooteca akee?*
Does one have to be a member?	É necessário ser membro? *eh necessaryoo sair membroo?*
Where can I find a good nightclub around here?	Onde é que há um bom clube nocturno aqui? *ond eh kuh ah oom bom cloob notoornoo akee?*

Is it evening wear only? _____ É obrigatório traje de cerimónia?
eh obreegatoryoo trarj duh cerimonnia?

Should I/we dress up? _ É aconselhável traje a preceito?
eh aconselyarvel trarj ah presaytoo?

What time does the _____ show start? A que horas começa o show?
ah kay orash coomessa oo show?

When's the next _____ soccer match? Quando é o próximo jogo de futebol?
cuarndoo eh oo prosseemoo jogoo duh footebol?

Who's playing? _____ Quem é que vai jogar?
caim eh kuh vy joogar?

I'd like an escort for_____ tonight. Could you arrange that for me? Queria ter um/uma acompanhante para hoje a noite. Pode tratar-me disto?
kerria tair oom/ooma acompanyant parra oarje a noyt. pod tratar muh deeshtoo?

11.3 Booking tickets

We'd like to book...	Queríamos reservar... *kerriamoosh rezairvar...*
– seats in the stalls	Queríamos reservar...lugares na plateia *kerriamoosh rezairvar...loogaresh na plataya*
– seats on the balcony	Queríamos reservar...lugares no balcão *kerriamoosh rezairvar...loogaresh noo balcow*
– a table at the front	Queríamos reservar uma mesa à frente *kerriamoosh rezairvar ooma mayza ah frent*
– seats in the centre	Queríamos reservar...lugares a meio *kerriamoosh rezairvar...loogaresh ah mayoo*
– seats at the back	Queríamos reservar...lugares atrás *kerriamoosh rezairvar...loogaresh atraj*
Could I book...seats for the...o'clock performance?	Posso reservar...lugares para a sessão das...? *possoo resairvar...loogaresh parra a sessow dash...?*
Are there any tickets left for tonight?	Ainda há bilhetes para esta noite? *ayeenda ah beelyetsch parra eshta noyt?*
How much is a ticket?	Quanto custa um bilhete? *cuarntoo cooshta oom beelyet?*
When can I pick the tickets up?	Quando é que posso levantar os bilhetes? *cuarndoo eh kuh possoo levantaroosh beelyetsch?*

I've got a reservation___ Reservei
resairvay

My name's... _____ O meu nome é...
oo mayoo nom eh...

Para que sessão é que deseja reservar?	Which performance do you want to book for?
Onde é que deseja se sentar?	Where would you like to sit?
Está esgotado	Everything's sold out
Só há lugares de pé	We've only got standing spaces left
Só há lugares no balcão	We've only got balcony seats left
Só há lugares na geral	We've only got seats left in the gallery
Só há lugares na plateia	We've only got stalls seats left
Só há lugares à frente	We've only got seats left at the front
Só há lugares atrás	We've only got seats left at the back
Quantos lugares deseja?	How many seats would you like?
Tem de levantar os bilhetes antes das...horas	You'll have to pick up the tickets before...o'clock
Posso ver os seus bilhetes?	Tickets, please
Este é o seu lugar	This is your seat
Estâo em lugares errados	You're in the wrong seats

12.1 Sporting questions

Where can we... _____ around here?	Onde é que podemos...aqui?
	ond eh kuh poodaymooz...akee?
Is there a... _____ nearby?	Há um...perto daqui?
	ah oom...pairtoo dackee?
Can I hire a...here? ____	Posso alugar um/uma...aqui?
	possoo aloogar oom/ooma...akee?
Can I take...lessons? ___	Posso ter lições de...?
	possoo tair leesoynsh duh...?
How much is it per ____ hour/per day/a turn?	Quanto custa por hora/dia/vez?
	cuarntoo cooshta por ora/deeah/vaij?
Do I need a permit?____	É preciso uma licença?
	eh preseezoo ooma leesensa?
Where can I get _____ the permit?	Onde é que posso tirar a licença?
	ond eh kuh possoo teerar a leesensa?

12.2 By the waterfront

Is it a long way _____ (by foot) to the sea?	É muito longe (a pé) daqui ao mar?
	eh mueentoo lonj (ah peh) dakee ow mar?
Is there...nearby? _____	Há um/uma...perto daqui?
	ah akee oom/ooma...pairtoo dackee?
– an outdoor/indoor/ ___ public swimming pool nearby?	Há uma piscina perto daqui?
	ah ooma peeshseena pairtoo dackee?
– a sandy beach _____ nearby?	Há aqui uma praia de areia perto?
	ah akee ooma prya di araya pairtoo?
– a nudist beach _____ nearby?	Há uma praia de naturistas perto daqui?
	ah ooma prya duh natooreeshtash pairtoo dackee?
– a quay nearby? _____	Há um cais perto daqui?
	ah oom kysh pairtoo dackee?

Are there any rocks here?	Há rochas aqui?
ah roshash akee?	
When's high/low tide?	Quando é a maré cheia/a maré vazia?
	cuarndoo eh a maray shaya/a maray vazeeah?
What's the water temperature?	Qual é a temperatura da água?
	cuarl eh a temperatoora da agwar?
Is it (very) deep here?	Aqui é (muito) fundo?
	akee eh mweentoo foondoo?
Can I reach the ground here?	Aqui tenho pé?
	akee tenyoo peh?
Is it safe to swim here?	É seguro nadar aqui (para as crianças)?
	eh segooroo nadar akee (parra ash creansash)?
Are there any currents?	Há correntes?
	ah coorentesh?
Are there any rapids/ waterfalls in this river?	Este rio tem rápidos/cataratas?
	esht reeoo taim rappeedoosh/cataratash?
What does that flag/ buoy mean?	O que significa aquela bandeira/bóia?
	oo kuh signeefeeca akela bandayra/boya?
Is there a life guard on duty here?	Há aqui um salva-vidas?
	ah akee oom salva-veedash?
Are dogs allowed here?	São permitidos cães aqui?
	sow permeeteedoosh caynz akee?
Is camping on the beach allowed?	Pode-se acampar aqui na praia?
	pod suh acampar akee na prya?
Is it permitted to build a fire here?	Pode-se fazer uma fogueira aqui?
	pod suh fazair ooma foogayra akee?

Perigo	É proibido pescar	É proibido nadar
Danger	No fishing	No swimming
É permitido pescar	É proibido fazer surf	Só com licença
Fishing allowed	No surfing	Permits only

13.1 Call (fetch) the doctor

Could you call/fetch a __ doctor quickly, please?

Podia chamar/ir buscar um médico depressa, se faz favor?
poodia shamar/eer booshcar oom maydeecoo, suh faj favvor?

When does the doctor _ have surgery?

Quando é a consulta do médico?
cuarndoo eh a consoolta doo meydeecoo?

When can the doctor___ come?

Quando é que o médico pode vir?
cuarndoo eh kuh oo meydeecoo pod veer?

I'd like to make an _____ appointment to see the doctor

Podia marcar-me uma consulta no médico?
poodia marcar muh ooma consoolta noo meydeecoo?

I've got an _____ appointment to see the doctor at...

Tenho uma consulta no médico às...horas
tenyoo ooma consoolta noo meydeecoo az...orash

Which doctor/chemist___ has night/weekend duty?

Que médico/farmácia tem serviço nocturno/de fim de semana?
kuh meydeecoo/farmassia taim sairveesoo notoornoo/duh feem duh semarna?

13.2 Patient's ailments

I don't feel well _____	Não me sinto bem
	now muh seentoo baim
I'm dizzy _____	Tenho tonturas
	tenyoo tontoorash
I feel ill _____	Sinto-me doente
	seentoo muh dooent
I feel sick _____	Sinto-me enjoado
	seento muh enjooardoo
I've got a cold _____	Sinto-me constipado
	seento muh conshteepardoo
It hurts here _____	Dói-me aqui
	doy muh akee
I've been throwing up __	Vomitei
	voomeetay
I've got a headache _____	Tenho dor de cabeca
	tenyoo door duh cabaysa
I'm running a _____ temperature of...degrees	Tenho...graus de febre
	tenyoo...growsh duh febre
I've been stung by _____ a wasp	Fui picado por uma abelha
	fwee peecardoo por ooma abelya
I've been stung by an __ insect	Fui picado por um insecto
	fwee picardoo por oom eensetoo
I've been bitten by _____ a dog	Fui mordido por um cão
	fwee mordeedoo por oom cow
I've been stung by _____ a jellyfish	Fui mordido por uma alforreca
	fwee mordeedoo por ooma alfooreka
I've been bitten by _____ a snake	Fui mordido por uma cobra
	fwee mordeedoo por ooma cobbra
I've been bitten by _____ an animal	Fui mordido por um bicho
	fwee mordeedoo por oom beeshoo
I've cut myself _____	Cortei-me
	cortay muh

I've burned myself _____	Queimei-me
	kaymay muh
I've grazed myself _____	Fiz um arranhão
	feez oom aranyow
I've had a fall _____	Caí
	ky
I've sprained my ankle _	Torci o tornozelo
	torsee oo toornnzeloo
I've come for a _____ morning-after pill	Venho pedir uma pílula `morning-after' *venyoo pedeer ooma peeloola 'morning-after'*

13.3 The consultation

O que tem?	What seems to be the problem?
Há quanto tempo sofre disto?	How long have you had these symptoms?
Já teve isto antes?	Have you had this trouble before?
Que febre tem?	How high is your temperature?
Podia despir-se, se faz favor?	Get undressed, please
Podia despir-se da cintura para cima?	Strip to the waist
Pode despir-se ali	You can undress there
Puxe a manga esquerda/direita para cima?	Roll up your left/right sleeve
Deite-se aqui	Lie down here
Isto faz-lhe doer?	Does this hurt?
Respire fundo	Breathe deeply
Abra a boca	Open your mouth

É alérgico a qualquer coisa?	Do you have any allergies?
Toma medicamentos?	Are you on any medication?
Faz qualquer dieta?	Are you on any sort of diet?
Está grávida?	Are you pregnant?
Está vacinado contra o tétano?	Have you had a tetanus vaccination?
Não é nada de grave	It's nothing serious
Partiu o/a...	You've broken your...
Magoou o/a...	You've bruised your...
Estalou o/a...	You've split your...
Tem uma inflamação	You've got an inflammation
Tem uma apendicite	You've got appendicitis
Tem uma bronquite	You've got bronchitis
Tem uma doença venérea	You've got a venereal disease
Tem uma gripe	You've got the flu
Teve um ataque cardíaco	You've had a heart attack
Tem uma infecção (provocada por um vírus/uma bactéria)	You've got an infection (viral/bacteria)

Patient's medical history

I'm a diabetic	Sofro de diabetes
	sofroo duh deeabetsh
I have a heart condition	Sofro do coração
	sofroo doo coorasow
I have asthma	Sofro de asma
	sofroo di ajma
I'm allergic to...	Sou alérgico a...
	soe alergeeco ah...
I'm...months pregnant	Estou grávida de...meses
	eshtoe graveeda duh...meyzesh

Tem uma infecção pulmonar	You've got pneumonia
Tem uma úlcera	You've got an ulcer
Distendeu um músculo	You've pulled a muscle
Tem uma infecção na vagina	You've got a vaginal infection
Tem uma intoxicação de alimentos	You've got food poisoning
Apanhou uma insolação	You've got sunstroke
É alérgico a...	You're allergic to...
Está grávida	You're pregnant
Tem de fazer análises ao sangue/à urina/às fezes	You'll need to have your blood/urine/stools tested
Tem de levar pontos	It needs stitching
Tem de ir a um especialista/ para o hospital	I'm referring you to a specialist/sending you to hospital
Tem de tirar radiografias	You'll need to have some x-rays taken
Pode aguardar ainda na sala de espera, se faz favor?	Could you wait in the waiting room, please?
Tem de ser operado	You'll need an operation

I'm on a diet _____	Estou de dieta *eshtoe duh deeayta*
I'm on medication/the pill	Tomo medicamentos/a pílula *tomoo medeecamentoosh/a peeloola*
I've had a heart attack once before	Já tive outro ataque cardíaco *jah teev ohtroo atak cardeeacoo*
I've had a...operation___	Fui operado de... *fwee operardoo duh...*
I've been ill recently____	Estive doente recentemente *eshteev dooent recentement*
I've got an ulcer _____	Tenho uma úlcera *tenyoo ooma oolsera*
I've got my period _____	Estou com a menstruação *eshtoe com a menshtrooasow*

The diagnosis

Is it contagious? _____	É contagioso?
	eh contajiozoo?
How long do I have to__ stay...?	Quanto tempo tenho de ficar...?
	cuarntoo tempoo tenyoo duh feecar...?
– in bed _____	Quanto tempo tenho de ficar de cama?
	cuarntoo tempoo tenyoo duh feecar duh camma?
– in hospital_____	Quanto tempo tenho de ficar no hospital?
	cuarntoo tempoo tenyoo duh feecar noo oshpeetal?
Do I have to go on _____ a special diet?	Tenho de fazer alguma dieta?
	tenyoo duh fazair algooma diayta?
Am I allowed to travel? _	Posso viajar?
	possoo veajar?
Can I make a new _____ appointment?	Posso marcar outra consulta?
	possoo marcar ohtra conssoolta?
When do I have to _____ come back?	Quando é que tenho de voltar?
	cuarndoo eh kuh tenyoo duh voltar?
I'll come back _____ tomorrow	Volto amanhã
	voltoo armanyar

Volte amanhã/daqui a...dias   Come back tomorrow/in...days' time

13.4 Medication and prescriptions

How do I take this ____ medicine?	**Como é que tenho de tomar este medicamento?** *coemoo eh kuh tenyoo duh toomar esht medeecamentoo?*
How many capsules/___ drops/injections/ spoonfuls/tablets each time?	**Quantas cápsulas/gotas/injecções/ colheres/comprimidos de uma vez?** *cuarntash capsoolash/gottash, eenjecsoynsh/coolyairesh/compreemeedo sh di ooma vej?*
How many times a day?	**Quantas vezes por dia?** *cuarntash vayzesh por deeah?*
I've forgotten my ____ medication. At home I take...	**Esqueci-me dos meus medicamentos. Costumo tomar...** *eshkessee muh doosh mayoosh meydeecamentoosh. coshtoomoo toomar...*
Could you make out a__ prescription for me?	**Podia passar-me uma receita?** *poodia passar muh ooma ressayta?*

Receito-lhe um antibiótico/ xarope/sedativo/analgésico	I'm prescribing antibiotics/a mixture/a tranquillizer/pain killers
Tem de descansar	You need to rest
Tem de ficar dentro de casa	Stay indoors
Tem de ficar na cama	Stay in bed

antes das refeições	durante...dias	...vezes por dia
before meals	for...days	...times a day
cápsulas	engolir inteiro	só para uso externo
capsules	swallow	only for external use
dissolver em água	whole	terminar a cura
dissolve in water	esfregar	finish the prescription
comprimidos	rub on	tomar
tablets	gotas	take
colheres (de	drops	este medicamento
sopa/de chá)	injecções	pode influenciar a
spoonfuls	injections	condução
(tablespoons/	pomada	this medication
teaspoons)	ointment	impairs your driving

13.5 At the dentist's

Do you know a good___ dentist?	Conhece um bom dentista?
	coonyess oom bom denteeshta?
Could you make a _____ dentist's appointment for me? It's urgent	Podia marcar-me uma consulta no dentista? É urgente
	poodia marcar muh ooma consoolta noo denteeshta? Eh oorgent
Can I come in today, ___ please?	Podia ser ainda hoje?
	poodia sair ayeenda oarje?
I have (terrible) _____ toothache	Tenho (imensa) dor de dentes
	tenyoo (eemensa) door duh dentesh
Could you prescribe/___ give me a painkiller?	Podia receitar-me um analgésico?
	poodia ressaytar muh oom analjezzeecoo?
One of my teeth _____ has cracked	Partiu-se um dos meus dentes
	partyoo suh oom doosh mayoosh dentesh
My filling's come out ___	O chumbo do dente caiu
	oo choomboo doo dent cayoo

I've got a cracked ____ crown	Partiu-se a coroa *partyoo suh ah coroah*
I'd like/I don't want a___ local anaesthetic	Gostava/não gostava de anestesia local *goshtarv/now goshtarv duh aneshtezia loocal*
Can you do a makeshift repair job?	Podia fazer um arranjo provisório? *poodia fazair oom arranjoo prooveesoryoo?*
I don't want this tooth___ pulled	Não quero que arranque este dente *now cairoo kuh arrank esht dent*
My dentures are broken. Can you fix them?	A minha dentadura partiu-se. Podia arranjá-la? *a meenya dentadoora partyoo suh. Poodia arranjar la?*

Que dente lhe dói?	Which tooth hurts?
Tem um abcesso	You've got an abscess
Tem de fazer um tratamento ao nervo	I'll have to do a root canal
Vou fazer uma anestesia local	I'm giving you a local anaesthetic
Tenho de chumbar/tirar/limar este dente	I'll have to fill/pull/file this tooth
Tenho de brocar	I'll have to drill
Abra a boca	Open your mouth
Feche a boca	Close your mouth
Bochechar	Rinse
Ainda sente dores?	Does it hurt still?

14

In trouble

14.1 Asking for help

Help! _____	**Socorro!**
	socooroo!
Fire! _____	**Fogo!**
	foegoo!
Police! _____	**Polícia!**
	pooleecia!
Quick! _____	**Depressa!**
	depressa!
Danger! _____	**Perigo!**
	pereegoo!
Watch out! _____	**Atenção!**
	atensow
Stop! _____	**Páre!**
	parah!
Be careful! _____	**Cuidado!**
	cweedardoo
Don't! _____	**Não faça isso!**
	now fassa eessoo!
Let go! _____	**Largar!**
	largar!
Stop that thief! _____	**Apanhe o ladrão!**
	apanya oo ladrow!
Could you help me, ____ please?	**Podia ajudar-me?**
	poodia ajoodar muh?
Where's the police station/emergency exit/fire escape?	**Onde é a polícia/a saída de emergência/ a escada de incêndios?**
	ond eh a pooleecia/a sayeeda di emerjencia/a eshcarda di eencendyoosh?
Where's the nearest fire extinguisher?	**Onde está o extintor?**
	ond eshtah oo eshteentor?
Call the fire brigade! ____	**Chame os bombeiros!**
	shamma oosh bombayroosh!
Call the police! _____	**Telefone à polícia**
	telefon ah pooleecia!

Call an ambulance! _____	Chame uma ambulância
	shamma ooma amboolancia
Where's the nearest_____ phone?	Onde é o telefone?
	ond eh oo telefon?
Could I use your _____ phone?	Posso usar o seu telefone?
	possoo oozar oo sayoo telefon?
What's the emergency _ number?	Qual é o número de urgência?
	cuarl eh oo noomeroo duh oorjensia?
What's the number for _ the police?	Qual é o número da polícia?
	cuarl eh oo noomeroo da pooleecia?

14.2 Loss

I've lost my purse/ _____ wallet	Perdi o meu porta-moedas/a minha carteira
	pairdee oo mayoo porta mooaydash/a meenya cartayra
I lost my...yesterday_____	Ontem esqueci-me do meu/da minha...
	ontaim eshkecee muh doo mayoo/da meenya...
I left my...here _____	Deixei aqui o meu/a minha...
	dayshay akee oo mayoo/a meenya...
Did you find my...? _____	Encontrou o meu/a minha...?
	encontroe oo mayoo/a meenya...?
It was right here _____	Estava aqui
	eshtarva akee
It's quite valuable _____	É bastante valioso
	eh bashtant valiozoo
Where's the lost _____ property office?	Onde é a secção de perdidos e achados?
	ond eh a seksow duh pairdeedoos e achardoosh?

There's been an _____ accident	Houve um acidente
	ohve oom asseedent
Someone's fallen into __ the water	Caiu uma pessoa na água
	cayoo ooma pessoa nah agwa
There's a fire _____	Há fogo
	ha foegoo
Is anyone hurt?_____	Alguém está ferido?
	algaim eshtah fereedoo?
No one's been injured __	Não há feridos
	now ah fereedoosh
Some people have been injured	Há alguns feridos
	ah algoons fereedoosh
There's still someone in the car/train	Ainda há uma pessoa no carro/comboio
	ayeenda hah ooma pessoa noo cahroo/comboyoo
It's not too bad. Don't __ worry	Não é nada. Não se preocupe
	now eh narda. Now suh preeocoop
Don't touch anything___	Não mexa em nada
	now mesha aim narda
I want to talk to the ____ police first	Queria falar primeiro com a polícia
	kerria falar preemayroo com a pooleecia
I want to take a_____ photo first	Primeiro quero tirar uma fotografia
	preemayroo cairoo teerar ooma fotografeea
Here's my name _____ and address	Tem aqui o meu nome e morada
	taim akee oo mayoo nom ee moorarda
Could I have your_____ name and address?	Podia dar-me o seu nome e morada?
	poodia dar muh oo sayoo nom e moorarda?
Could I see some_____ identification/your insurance papers?	Posso ver os seus documentos de identificação/o seu seguro?
	possoo vair oosh sayoosh docoomentoosh di eedentifeecasow/oo sayoo segooroo?
Will you act as a_____ witness?	Quer ser testemunha?
	care sair teshtemoonya?

I need to know the ___ details for the insurance	Tenho de saber os dados para o seguro
	tenyoo duh sabbair oosh dardoosh parra oo segooroo
Are you insured? _____	Tem um seguro?
	taim oom segooroo?
Third party or _____ comprehensive?	Contra terceiros ou contra todos os riscos?
	contra tairsayroosh o contra toedoos oosh reeshcoosh?
Could you sign here, ___ please?	Podia assinar aqui?
	poodia asseenar akee?

14.4 Theft

I've been robbed _____	Fui roubado
	fwee roobardoo
My...has been stolen ___	Roubaram-me o meu/a minha...
	roobaram muh oo mayoo/a meenya...
My car's been _____ broken into	Assaltaram-me o carro
	assalltaram muh oo cahroo

14.5 Missing person

I've lost my child/_____ grandmother	Perdi o meu filho (a minha filha)/a minha avó
	pairdee oo mayoo feelyoo (a meenya feelya)/a meenya avoh
Could you help me ____ find him/her?	Podia ajudar-me a procurar?
	poodia ajoodar muh a procoorar?
Have you seen a _____ small child?	Viu uma criança pequena?
	veeoo ooma creeansa peekayna?
He's/she's...years old __	Ele/ela tem...anos
	el/alla taim...arnoosh

He's/she's got _____ short/long/blond/red/ brown/black/grey/ straight/curly/frizzy hair	Ele/ela tem cabelo curto/comprido/louro/ ruivo/castanho/preto/grisalho/liso/ encaracolado/frizado *el/ella taim cabayloo coortoo/rooeevoo/cashtanyoo/ praytoo/greesalyoo/leezoo/ aincarracoolardoo/freezardoo*
in a ponytail_____	tem rabo de cavalo *taim rarboo duh cavarloo*
in plaits_____	tem tranças *taim transash*
in a bun _____	tem um carrapito *taim oom carrapeetoo*
He's/she's got _____ blue/brown/green eyes	Os olhos são azuis/castanhos/verdes *ooz olyoosh sow azweesh/castanyoosh/vairdsh*
He's wearing swimming trunks/mountaineering boots	Tem uns calções de banho vestidos/uns sapatos de alpinismo calçados *taim unsh calsoynsh de bahnyoo veshteedoosh/unsh sapartoosh di alpeeneejmoo calsardoosh*
with/without glasses/ a bag	com/sem óculos/saco *com/saim occooloosh/sarcoo*
tall/short_____	grande/pequeno *grand/peekaynoo*
This is a photo of _____ him/her	Esta fotografia é dele/dela *eshta fotoografeea eh del/della*
He/she must be lost ___	Com certeza ele/ela se perdeu *com sairtayza el/ella suh pairdayoo*

14.6 The police

An arrest

I don't speak _____ Portuguese	Não falo português *now faloo poortoogayj*
I didn't see that sign ___	Não vi aquele sinal *now vee akel seenal*
I don't understand _____ what it says	Não compreendo o que significa *now comprayendoo oo kuh seegneefeeca*
I was only doing... _____ kilometres an hour	Só vinha a...km por hora *soh veenya a...km poor ora*
I'll have my car checked	Vou levar o meu carro à oficina *voe levvar oo mayoo cahro ah offeeseena*
I was blinded by _____ oncoming lights	Fiquei encadeado pelos faróis em sentido contrário *feekay encaddeardoo peloosh faroysh aim senteedoo contraryoo*

Os seus documentos, se faz favor	Your registration papers, please
Excedeu a velocidade máxima	You were speeding
Está mal estacionado	You're not allowed to park here
Não pôs dinheiro no parquímetro	You haven't put money in the meter
As luzes não funcionam	Your lights aren't working
É uma multa de...euros	That's a...euros fine
Quer pagar agora?	Do you want to pay on the spot?
Tem de pagar agora	You'll have to pay on the spot

At the police station

I want to report a _____ collision/missing person/rape	Venho declarar uma colisão/um desaparecimento/uma violação *venyoo declarar ooma cooleesow/oom dezaparessimentoo/ooma veeoolasow*
Could you make out ____ a report, please?	Podia fazer um relatório, se faz favor? *poodia fazair oom relatoryoo, suh faj favvor?*
Could I have a copy ____ for the insurance?	Posso levar uma cópia para o seguro? *possoo levvar ooma copia parra oo segooroo?*
I've lost everything_____	Perdi tudo *pairdee toodoo*
I've no money at all. ____ I'm desperate	Não tenho dinheiro nenhum. Estou desesperado *now tenyoo deenyayroo nenyoom. eshtoe deseshperardoo*
Can you lend me some_ money?	Pode emprestar-me algum dinheiro? *poodia empreshtar muh algoom deenyayroo?*

Onde é que aconteceu?	Where did it happen?
O que é que perdeu?	What's missing?
O que é que foi roubado?	What's been taken?
Tem os seus documentos de identificação?	Do you have some identification?
A que horas aconteceu?	What time did it happen?
Quem são os outros?	Who are the others?
Há testemunhas?	Are there any witnesses?
Preencha isto, se faz favor	Fill this out, please
Assinar aqui, se faz favor	Sign here, please
Quer um intérprete?	Do you want an interpreter?

English	Portuguese
I'd like an interpreter ___	Queria um intérprete *kerria oom eentairpret*
I'm innocent _____	Estou inocente *eshtoe eenoosent*
I don't know anything __ about it	Não sei nada *now say narda*
I want to speak to _____ someone from the British consulate	Queria falar com alguém do Consulado Britânico *kerria falar com algaim doo consoolardoo breetaneecoo*
I want to speak to _____ someone from the British embassy	Queria falar com alguém da Embaixada Britânica *kerria falar com algaim da embysharda breetaneeca*
I want a lawyer _____ who speaks English	Queria um advogado que fale inglês *kerria oom advoogardoo kuh fal eenglayj*

Word list English – Portuguese

● **This word list** is meant to supplement previous chapters. In a number of cases, words not contained in this list can be found elsewhere in this book, namely in the lists of the parts of the car, the bicycle and the tent. Many food terms can be found in the Portuguese–English list in 4.7

A

about	acerca de	asserca duh
above, up	em cima	aim seema
abroad	estrangeiro	eshtranjayroo
accident	acidente	assident
adder	víbora	veebora
addition	soma	somma
address	morada	mooradah
adhesive tape	fita cola	feeta colla
admission	entrada	entrarda
admission price	preço de entrada	praysoo duh entrarda
advice	conselho	consellyoo
after	depois	depoysh
afternoon	tarde	tard
aftershave	loção para a barba	loosow parra ah barba
again	novamente	novvament
against	contra	contra
age	idade	eedarde
Aids	Sida	seeda
air conditioning	ar condicionado	ar condeesionardoo
air mattress	colchão inflável	colchow eenflarvel
air sickness bag	saco para enjôo	sarcoo parra ainjoh-oo
aircraft	avião	avviow
airport	aeroporto	airoopoortoo
alarm	alarme	alarm
alarm clock	despertador	deshpairtadoor
alcohol	âlcool	alcoooll
allergic	alérgico	alergeecoo

alone	só	*soh*
always	sempre	*sempra*
ambulance	ambulância	*amboolancia*
amount	quantia, quantidade	*quarnteeah, quarnteedard*
amusement park	parque de diversões	*park duh deevaisoynsh*
anaesthetize	anestesiar	*aneshteziar*
anchovy	anchovas	*anshovvash*
angry	zangado	*zangardoo*
animal	animal	*animarl*
ankle	tornozelo	*tornoozelloo*
answer	resposta	*reshposhta*
ant	formiga	*formeega*
antibiotics	antibióticos	*antibeeoteecoosh*
antifreeze	anticongelante	*anticongellant*
antique	antigo	*anteegoo*
antiques	antiguidades	*anteegweedardesh*
anus	ânus	*arnoosh*
apartment	apartamento	*apartamentoo*
aperitif	aperitivo	*aperiteevoo*
apologies	desculpas	*descoolpash*
apple	maçã	*massar*
apple juice	sumo de maçã	*soomoo duh massar*
apple pie	tarte de maçã	*tarte duh massar*
appointment	consulta	*consoolta*
apricot	alperce	*alpairce*
April	abril	*abreel*
architecture	arquitectura	*arkeetetoora*
area	arredores	*arredoresh*
arm	braço	*brarsoo*
arrange	combinar	*combeenar*
arrive	chegar	*sheggar*
arrow	seta	*setta*
art	arte	*art*
artery	artéria	*arterrya*
artichokes	alcachofras	*alcashoffrash*
article	artigo	*arteegoo*
artificial respiration	respiração artificial	*reshpeerasow arteefeecial*

ashtray	cinzeiro	*seenzayroo*
ask	perguntar	*pairgoontar*
ask	pedir	*pedeer*
asparagus	espargos	*eshpargoosh*
aspirin	aspirina	*ashpeereena*
assault	assalto	*assaltoo*
at home	em casa	*aim carza*
at last	afinal	*afeenal*
at night	à noite	*ah noyt*
at the back	atrás	*atraj*
at the front	à frente	*ah frent*
at the latest	no mais tardar	*noo mysh tardar*
aubergine	beringela	*berringella*
August	agosto	*agoshtoo*
automatic	automático	*owtoomateecoo*
automatically	automaticamente	*owtoomateecament*
autumn	outono	*ohtonoo*
awake	acordado	*acordardoo*
awning	toldo	*toldoo*

B

baby's bottle	biberão	*beeberow*
baby	bebé	*baybay*
baby car-seat	cadeira para bébé	*caddayra parra baybay*
baby food	comida para bébé	*comeeda parra baybay*
babysitter	babysitter	*baybeeseetair*
back	costas	*coshtash*
bacon	toucinho	*toosseenyoo*
bad	mau	*mow*
bad/off	estragado	*eshtragardoo*
bag (plastic)	saco (de plástico)	*sarcoo duh plashteecoo*
baker	padeiro	*paddayroo*
balcony (theatre)	balcão	*balcow*
balcony (of building)	varanda	*varanda*
ball	bola	*bolla*
ballet	ballet	*ballay*

ballpoint pen	esferográfica	*eshferoografeeca*
banana	banana	*bananna*
bandage	ligadura	*leegadoura*
bank (river)	margem	*marjaim*
bank	banco	*bancoo*
bar (café)	café	*cafay*
bar (drinks' cabinet)	bar	*bar*
barbecue	churrasco	*shoorashcoo*
bath	banho	*barnyoo*
bath foam	espuma de banho	*eshpooma duh barnyoo*
bath towel	toalha de banho	*tooalya duh barnyoo*
bath-tub	banheira	*banyayra*
bathing cap	touca de banho	*toeca duh barnyoo*
bathing suit	fato de banho	*fartoo duh barnyoo*
bathroom	casa de banho	*carza duh banyoo*
battery	pilha	*peelya*
battery	bateria	*batareeya*
be bored	aborrecer-se	*abooressair-suh*
be careful!	cuidado!	*cweedardoo*
be foggy	fazer nevoeiro	*fazzair nevooayroo*
be hungry	ter fome	*tair fom*
be in love with	estar namorado com	*eshtar namorardoo com*
be lost	perder-se	*pairdair-se*
be missing	faltar	*faltar*
be mistaken	enganar-se	*ainganar-suh*
beach	praia	*prya*
beautiful	lindo/belo	*leendoo/ bella*
beauty parlour	salão de beleza	*salow duh bellayza*
bed	cama	*camma*
bee	abelha	*abellya*
beef	carne de vaca	*carn duh varca*
beer	cerveja	*sairvayja*
beetroot	beterraba	*betterrarb*
begin	começar	*coomessar*
beginner	principiante	*preenseepeeant*
behind	atrás	*atraj*
belt	cinto	*seentoo*

beret	boina	*booeena*
berth	couchete	*cooshet*
better	melhor	*melyor*
bicarbonate of soda	bicarbonato de sódio	*beecarboonartoo duh sohdew*
bicycle	bicicleta	*beeseecletta*
bicycle pump	bomba de bicicleta	*bomba duh beeseecletta*
bicycle repair workshop	oficina de bicicletas	*offiseena duh beeseeclettash*
bikini	biquini	*bee-kee-nee*
bill	conta	*conta*
billiards, to play	jogar bilhar	*joogar beelyar*
birthday	aniversário	*anneevairsareeyoo*
birthday, to have a...	fazer anos	*fazzair arnoosh*
biscuit	biscoito	*beeshcoytoo*
bite	morder	*mordair*
bitter	amargo	*amargoo*
black	preto	*pretoo*
bland	insêpido	*eenseepeedoo*
blanket	cobertor	*coobertor*
bleach (hair)	pintar de louro	*peentar duh loroo*
bleeding nose	deitar sangue pelo nariz	*daytar sang peloo nareej*
blister	bolha	*bolya*
blond	louro	*loroo*
blood	sangue	*sang*
blood pressure	tensão arterial	*tensow arterrial*
blouse	blusa	*blooza*
blow dry	secar	*seccar*
blue	azul	*azool*
boat	barco	*barcoo*
body	corpo	*corpoo*
body milk	leite de beleza	*layt duh bellayza*
boiled	cozido	*coozeedoo*
boiled ham	fiambre	*feeambr*
bonbon	bombom	*bombom*
bone	osso	*ossoo*

bonnet	tampa do motor	*tampa doo motor*
book	livro	*leevroo*
book	reservar	*reservar*
booked	reservado	*reservardoo*
booking office	bilheteria	*beelyetareeah*
bookshop	livraria	*leevrareeah*
border	fronteira	*frontayra*
boring	monótono	*monotoonoo*
born/be born	nascido/nascer	*nashseedoo/nashayr*
borrow	pedir emprestado	*pedeer aimpreshtardoo*
botanical garden	jardim botânico	*jardeem bootaneecoo*
both	ambos	*amboosh*
bottlewarmer	aquecedor de biberões	*akessedor duh beeberoynsh*
bottle	garrafa	*garraffa*
box	caixa	*kysha*
box (theatre)	camarote	*cammarot*
boy	rapaz	*rapaj*
bra	soutien	*sootyan*
bracelet	pulseira	*poolsayra*
braised	estufado	*eshtoofardoo*
brake	travão	*travow*
brake fluid	líquido de travões	*leekeedoo duh travoynsh*
brake oil	óleo dos travões	*ollyoo doosh travoynsh*
brass	latão	*latow*
bread	pão	*pow*
break	partir	*parteer*
break-down	avaria do motor	*avaria doo motor*
breakdown service	pronto socorro	*prontoo socorroo*
breakfast	pequeno almoço	*peekaynoo almossoo*
breast	peito	*paytoo*
bridge	ponte	*pont*
bring	trazer	*trazair*
brochure	brochura	*brooshura*
broken	estragado	*eshtragardoo*
broken	partido	*parteedoo*
broth	caldo	*caldoo*

brother	irmão	*irmow*
brown	castanho	*cashtanyoo*
bruise	magoar	*magooar*
brush	escova	*eshcova*
bucket	balde	*balde*
bug	bicho	*beeshoo*
bugs	insectos	*eensetoosh*
building	edifício	*eedifeesyoo*
buoy	bóia	*boya*
bureau de change	casa de câmbio	*caza duh cambyoo*
burglary	assalto	*assaltoo*
burn	queimar	*kaymar*
burn	queimadura	*kaymadoora*
burnt	queimado	*kaymardoo*
bus station	estação de camionetas	*eshtasow duh camyoonetash*
bus stop	paragem de autocarro	*pararjaim duh owtoocahroo*
bus, coach	autocarro	*owtoocahroo*
business class	classe de negócios	*class duh negossyoosh*
business trip	viagem de negócios	*veearjaim duh negossioosh*
busy	atarefado/ocupado	*atarrefardoo/okoopardoo*
butcher	talho	*talyoo*
butter	manteiga	*mantayga*
buttered roll	pãozinho (com manteiga)	*powzeenyoo (com mantayga)*
button	botão	*bootow*
buy	comprar	*comprar*
by airmail	por correio aéreo	*por cooarayoo airayoo*

C

cabbage	couve	*cove*
cabin on ship	camarote	*camarot*
café	café	*cafay*
cake	bolinho	*boleenyoo*

cake	bolo	*boloo*
cake shop	pastelaria	*pastellereeah*
call	telefonar	*telefoonar*
called, to be	chamar-se	*shammar-suh*
camera	máquina fotográfica	*markeena fotografeeca*
camp	acampar	*acampar*
camp shop	loja	*lohja*
camp site	campismo	*campeejmoo*
camp site	parque de campismo	*park duh campeejmoo*
camp-fire	fogueira	*foogayra*
camper	carrinha de campismo	*careenya duh campeejmoo*
camping guide	guia de campismo	*gueeah duh campeejmoo*
camping permit	autorização de campismo	*owtoreezasow duh campeejmoo*
canal boat	barco de excursão	*barcoo di eshcoorsow*
cancel	anular	*anoolar*
candle	vela	*vella*
canoe	canoa	*canoah*
canoe	fazer canoagem	*fazzair canooarjaim*
car	automóvel	*owtoomohvel*
car	carruagem	*carruarjaim*
car deck	porão de veículos	*poorow duh vayeecooloosh*
car documents	documentos do carro	*docoomentoosh doo cahroo*
caravan	roulotte	*roolott*
cardigan	casaco	*cazarcoo*
carrot	cenoura	*senora*
cartridge	carga de película fotogrêfica	*carga duh peleecoola fottoograrfeeca*
cash desk	caixa	*kysha*
casino	casino	*cazzeenoo*
cassette	cassette	*cassett*
castle	castelo	*cashteloo*
cat	gato	*gartoo*
catalogue	catálogo	*catalogoo*

cathedral	catedral	*cataydral*
cauliflower	couveflor	*cove flor*
cave	gruta	*groota*
CD	disco compacto (CD)	*deeshcoo compactoo (sayday)*
celebrate	festejar	*feshtayjar*
cemetery	cemitério	*semmeeterryoo*
centimetre	centímetro	*senteemetroo*
central heating	aquecimento central	*akessimentoo centrarl*
centre	(no) meio	*(noo) mayoo*
centre	centro	*centroo*
chair	cadeira	*cadayra*
chambermaid	camareira	*camarayra*
champagne	champanhe	*shampanya*
change	alterar	*alterrar*
change	mudar	*moodar*
change (transit)	fazer transbordo	*fazzair transhbordoo*
change	trocar	*troocar*
change currency	trocar dinheiro	*troocar deenyayroo*
change the baby's nappy	mudar a fralda	*moodar ah fralda*
change the oil	mudar o óleo	*moodar oo ollyoo*
chapel	capela	*capella*
charter flight	vôo charter	*voe shartair*
chat up	paquerar	*pakerrar*
check	ver, controlar	*vair, comtroolar*
check in	fazer o checkin	*fazzair oo sheckeen*
cheers	à saúde	*ah sow-ood*
cheese (tasty, mild)	queijo (bem curado, mal curado)	*kayjoo (baim coorardoo, mal coorardoo)*
chef	cozinheiro-chefe	*coozeenyayroo chef*
chemist	farmácia	*farmassia*
cheque	cheque	*sheck*
cheque card	cartão de cheques	*cartow duh sheksh*
cherries	cerejas	*serayjash*
chess, play	jogar xadrez	*joogar jadrayj*

chewing gum	pastilha elástica/ chiclete	*pashteelya eelashteeca/ cheeclet*
chicken	galinha, frango	*galeenya, frangoo*
child	criança	*creeansa*
child's seat	cadeira para bicicleta	*cadayra parra beeseeecletta*
chilled	fresco	*freshcoo*
chin	queixo	*kayshoo*
chips	batatas fritas	*batartash freetash*
chocolate	chocolate	*shoocoolat*
choose	escolher	*eschoolyair*
chop	costeleta	*coshteletta*
christian name	nome	*nom*
church	igreja	*eegrayja*
church service	missa	*meessa*
cigar	charuto	*charootoo*
cigar shop	tabacaria	*tabacareeah*
cigarette	cigarro	*seegarroo*
circle	círculo	*seercooloo*
circus	circo	*seercoo*
city	cidade	*seedard*
city map	planta da cidade	*planta da seedard*
classical concert	concerto de música clássica	*consairtoo duh mooseeca classeeca*
clean	limpo	*leempoo*
clean, to	limpar	*leempar*
clearance	saldo	*saldoo*
closed	fechado	*feshardoo*
clothes	roupa	*roepa*
clothes hanger	cabide	*cabeed*
clothes pegs	molas para a roupa	*mollash parra ah roepa*
clothing	vestuário	*veshtooaryoo*
coat	casaco	*cazarcoo*
cockroach	barata	*barata*
cocoa	cacau	*cackow*
cod	bacalhau fresco	*bacalyow freshcoo*
coffee	café	*cafay*

coffee filter	filtro de café	*feeltroo duh cafay*
cognac	conhaque	*coonyack*
cold (to be)	frio	*freeoo*
cold (to have a)	constipação	*conshteepasow*
collarbone	clavícula	*claveecoola*
colleague	colega	*coolegga*
collision	acidente	*asseedent*
collision	colisão	*cooleezow*
cologne	água de colônia	*agwa duh collonia*
colour	cor	*cor*
colour pencils	lápis de cor	*larpeej duh coor*
colour TV	televisão a cores	*televeesow ah cooresh*
colouring book	livro para colorir	*leevroo parra coloreer*
comb	pente	*pent*
come	vir	*veer*
come back	regressar, voltar	*regressar, voltar*
compartment	compartimento	*compartimentoo*
complaint	dor	*door*
complaint	queixa	*kaysha*
complaints book	livro de reclamações	*leevroo duh reclammasoynsh*
completely	completamente	*completament*
compliment	cumprimento	*coomprimentoo*
compulsory	obrigatório	*obrigatoryoo*
concert	concerto	*consairtoo*
concert hall, theatre	teatro	*teeartroo*
concussion	concussão cerebral	*concoosow cerebral*
condensed milk	leite condensado	*layt condensardoo*
condom	preservativo	*presairvateevoo*
congratulate	felicitar	*feleeceetar*
connection	ligação	*leegasow*
constipation	prisão de ventre	*preezow duh ventre*
consulate	consulado	*consoolardoo*
consultation	consulta	*consoolta*
contact lens	lente de contacto	*lent duh contactoo*
contact lens solution	fluido para lentes de contacto	*flooidoo parra lentsh duh contactoo*

contagious	contagioso	*contajeeozoo*
contraceptive pill	pílula	*peeloola*
	anticoncepcional	*anttconcepseeoonarl*
cook	cozinheiro	*coozeenyayroo*
cook, to	cozinhar	*coozeenyar*
copper	cobre	*cobbre*
copy	cópia	*cohpia*
corkscrew	sacarolhas	*sacca rollyash*
corn flour	maizena	*myzenna*
corner	canto	*cantoo*
corner	esquina	*eshkeena*
correct	certo	*sairtoo*
correspond	corresponder	*cooreshpondair*
corridor	corredor	*cooredoor*
cot	cama de bebé	*camma duh baybay*
cotton	algodão	*algoodow*
cotton wool	algodão	*algoodow*
cough	tosse	*toss*
cough mixture	xarope para a tosse	*sharopp parra a toss*
country	país	*pyeej*
country	campoo	*campoo*
country code	indicativo do país	*eendeecateevoo*
courgette	courgete	*corjet*
cousin	primo/prima	*preemoo/preema*
crab	caranguejo	*carangayjoo*
cream	creme/natas	*crem/nartash*
credit card	cartão de crédito	*cartow duh credeetoo*
crisps	batatas fritas	*batartash freetash*
croissant	croissant	*croisson*
cross (the road)	atravessar	*atravessar*
crossing	travessia	*travessia*
crossing	passagem	*passarjaim*
cry	chorar	*shoorar*
cubic metre	metro cúbico	*metroo coobeecoo*
cucumber	pepino	*pepeenoo*
cuddly toy	boneco de peluche	*booneckoo duh peloosh*
cuff links	botões de punho	*bootoynsh duh poonyoo*

culottes	saia calça	*syah calsa*
cup	chávena	*sharvena*
curly	encaracolado	*aincarracoolardoo*
current	corrente	*coorent*
cushion	almofadinha	*almoffardeenya*
custard	creme	*crem*
customary	ê costume	*eh coshtoom*
customs	alfândega	*alfandegga*
customs	controle de alfândega	*controll di alfandegga*
cut	cortar	*cortar*
cutlery	talher	*talyair*
cycling	ciclismo	*seecleejmoo*

D

dairy	leiteria	*laytereeah*
damaged	danificado	*danifeecardoo*
dance	dançar	*dansar*
dandruff	caspa	*cashpa*
danger	perigo	*perreegoo*
dangerous	perigoso	*perrigozoo*
dark	escuro	*eshcooroo*
date	encontro	*aincontroo*
daughter	filha	*feelya*
day	dia	*deeah*
day before yesterday	anteontem	*antiontaim*
dead	morto	*mortoo*
decaffeinated	descafeinado	*deshcafaynardoo*
December	dezembro	*dezembroo*
deck chair	cadeira de praia	*cadayra duh prya*
declare (customs)	declarar	*declarar*
deep	profundo	*proofoondoo*
deep sea diving	mergulho	*mairgoolyoo*
deepfreeze	congelador	*conjellador*
degrees	graus	*graush*
delay	atraso	*atrarzoo*

delicatessen	charcutaria	*sharcootareeah*
delicious	saboroso	*saborohzoo*
delicious	delicioso	*delisseeohzoo*
dentist	dentista	*denteeshta*
dentures	dentadura	*dentadoora*
deodorant	desodorizante	*desodoreezant*
department	secção	*secksow*
department store	armazém	*armazaim*
departure	partida	*parteeda*
departure time	hora de partida	*ora duh parteeda*
depilatory cream	creme depilatório	*crem depeelatoryoo*
deposit	sinal	*seenal*
dessert	sobremesa	*sobremayza*
destination	destino	*deshteenoo*
destiny	destino	*deshteenoo*
develop	revelar	*revelar*
diabetic	diabético	*deeabeteecoo*
dial	marcar	*marcar*
dialling code	indicativo	*eendeecateevoo*
diamond	diamante	*deeamant*
diarrhoea	diarreia	*deearraya*
dictionary	dicionário	*deesionaryoo*
diesel	diesel	*deezel*
diesel oil	gasóleo	*gazollyoo*
diet	dieta	*deeayta*
difficulty	dificuldade	*deefeeculdard*
dining room	sala de jantar	*sarla duh jantar*
dining/buffet car	vagão restaurante	*vagow reshtowrant*
dinner	jantar	*jantar*
dinner jacket	smoking	*smockeeng*
direction	direcção	*deeressow*
directly	directo	*deerectoo*
dirty	sujo	*soojoo*
disabled	inválido	*eenvalleedoo*
disco	discoteca	*deeshcooteca*
discount	desconto	*deshcontoo*
dish	prato	*prartoo*

dish of the day	prato do dia	*prartoo doo deeah*
disinfectant	desinfectante	*dezeenfectant*
distance	distância	*deeshtarncia*
distilled water	água destilada	*agwa deshteelarda*
disturb	incomodar	*eencoomoodar*
disturbance	perturbação	*pairtoorbasow*
diving	mergulhar	*mairgoolyar*
diving board	prancha de saltos	*pransha duh saltoosh*
diving gear	equipamento para mergulhar	*ekeepamentoo parra mairgoolyar*
divorced	divorciado	*deevorceeardoo*
DIY shop	loja faça-você-mesmo	*loja fassa vossay mejmoo*
dizzy	tonto	*tontoo*
do	fazer	*fazzair*
doctor	médico	*mehdeecoo*
dog	cão	*cow*
doll	boneca	*booneca*
domestic	doméstico	*doomehsteecoo*
door	porta	*porta*
double bed	cama de casal	*camma duh cazal*
down	em baixo	*aim byshoo*
draught	corrente de ar	*coorent di ar*
dream	sonhar	*soonyar*
dress	vestido	*veshteedoo*
dressing gown	roupão	*roepow*
drink	bebida	*bebbeeda*
drink	beber	*bebbair*
drinking chocolate	leite com chocolate	*layt com shoocoolat*
drinking water	água potável	*agwa pootarvel*
drive	conduzir	*condoozeer*
drive	motorista	*motoreeshta*
driving licence	carta de condução	*carta duh condoosow*
drought	seca	*sayca*
dry	secar	*seccar*
dry	seco	*saycoo*
dry clean	limpar a seco	*leempar ah saycoo*

dry cleaner's	limpeza a seco	*leempayza ah saycoo*
dry shampoo	champô seco	*shampoh saycoo*
dummy	chupeta	*shoopeta*
during	durante	*doorant*
during the day	durante o dia	*doorant oo deeah*
duty free shop	loja franca	*loja franca*

E

ear	orelha/ouvido	*orelya/ohveedoo*
ear, nose and throat specialist	otorrinolaringo-logista	*otorreenoolareengo-loojeeshta*
earache	dor de ouvidos	*door duh oeveedoosh*
eardrops	gotas para os ouvidos	*gotash parra ooz oeveedoosh*
early	cedo	*saydoo*
earrings	brincos	*breencoosh*
earth	terra	*tehrah*
earthenware	cerâmica	*serrameeca*
east	este	*esht*
easy	fácil	*farseel*
eat	comer	*comair*
eczema	eczema	*eczma*
eel	enguia	*aingueeah*
egg	ovo	*ohvoo*
elastic band	elástico	*elashteecoo*
electric	eléctrico	*eletreecoo*
electricity	electricidade	*eletreesidard*
embassy	embaixada	*embysharda*
emergency brake	alarme	*alarm*
emergency exit	saída de emergência	*syeeda duh emairjensia*
emergency number	número de alarme	*noomeroo duh alarm*
emergency phone	telefone de emergência	*telefon duh emairjensia*
emergency triangle	triângulo de emergência	*treeangooloo duh emairjensia*
emery board	lima de unhas	*leema duh oonyash*

empty	vazio	*vazeeoo*
engaged	ocupado	*ocupardoo*
England	Inglaterra	*eenglaterra*
English, Englishman	inglês	*eenglayj*
enjoy	ter prazer	*tair prezzair*
entertainment (show) event	espectáculo	*espetarcooloo*
entertainment guide	revista de espectáculos	*reveeshta duh espetarcooloosh*
envelope	envelope	*envellop*
escort	acompanhante	*acompanyant*
evening (before 6pm)	tarde	*tard*
evening wear	traje de noite	*trarge duh noyt*
everything	tudo	*toodoo*
everywhere	por toda a parte	*por toeda ah part*
examine	examinar	*eezameenar*
excavations	escavações	*eshcavasoynsh*
excellent	óptimo	*otteemoo*
exchange	trocar	*troocar*
exchange rate	câmbio	*cambyoo*
excursion	excursão	*eshcoorsow*
exhibition	exposição	*eshpozisow*
exit	saida	*syeeda*
expenses	despesas	*deshpayzash*
expensive	caro	*caroo*
explain	explicar	*eeshpleecar*
express	comboio rápido	*comboyoo rapeedoo*
external	externo	*eeshtairnoo*
eye	olho	*olyoo*
eyedrops	gotas para os olhos	*gotash parra ooz olyoosh*
eyeshadow	sombra	*sombra*
eye specialist	oftalmologista	*oftalmolojeeshta*
eyeliner	lápis para os olhos	*larpeesh parra ooz olyoos*

face	cara	*cara*
factory	fábrica	*fabreeca*
fair	feira	*fayra*
fall	cair	*kyeer*
family	famÌlia	*fameelia*
famous	famoso	*famozoo*
far away	longe	*lonj*
farm	quinta	*keenta*
farmer	agricultor	*agreecooltor*
farmer's wife	mulher do agricultor	*moolyair do agreecooltor*
fashion	moda	*mohda*
fast	rápido	*rapeedoo*
father	pai	*pie*
fault	culpa	*coolpa*
fax, send a	enviar um fax	*enveear oom fax*
February	fevereiro	*fevverayroo*
feel	sentir	*senteer*
feel like	ter vontade	*tair vontard*
fence	vedação	*veddasow*
ferry	barco	*barcoo*
fever	febre	*febre*
fill a tooth	obturar um dente	*obtoorar oom dent*
fill out	preencher	*pree-enshair*
filling	obturaçâo	*obtoorasow*
film	rolo fotográfico	*rolloo fotoograrfeecoo*
film	filme	*feelm*
filter	filtro	*feeltroo*
find	achar	*ashar*
fine	multa	*moolta*
finger	dedo	*daydoo*
fire	fogueira	*foogayra*
fire	incêndio	*eensendyoo*
fire brigade	bombeiros	*bombayroosh*
fire escape	escada de emergência	*eshcarda duh emmairjensia*

fire extinguisher	extintor	*eshteentor*
first	primeiro	*preemayroo*
first aid	primeiros socorros	*preemayroosh socorroosh*
first class	primeira classe	*preemayra class*
fish, to	pescar	*peshcar*
fish	peixe	*paysh*
fishing rod	cana de pesca	*carna duh peshca*
fit	assentar	*assentar*
fitness centre	centro de manutenção física	*sentroo duh manootensow feeseeca*
fitness training	treino de manutenção física	*traynoo duh manootensow feeseeca*
fitting room	gabinete de prova	*gabeenet duh provva*
fix/stick	colar/consertar	*coollar/consairtar*
flag	bandeira	*bandayra*
flash bulb	lâmpada do flash	*lamparda doo flash*
flash cube	flash em cubo	*flash aim cooboo*
flea market	feira da ladra	*fayra da ladra*
flight	vôo	*voe*
flight number	número do vôo	*noomeroo duh voe*
flood	inundação	*eenoondasow*
floor (building)	andar	*andar*
flour	farinha	*fareenya*
flyover	viaduto	*veeadootoo*
fly (insect)	mosca	*moshca*
fly (verb)	voar	*vooar*
fog	nevoeiro	*nevooayroo*
folding caravan	atrelado	*atrelardoo*
folkloric	folclórico	*folclorreecoo*
follow	seguir	*segear*
food	alimento	*allymentoo*
food poisoning	intoxicação alimentar	*eentoxeecasow allimentar*
foot	pé	*peh*
for	para	*parra*
for hire	aluga-se	*alooga-suh*
forbidden	proibido	*prooeebeedoo*

forehead	testa	*teshta*
foreign	estrangeiro	*eshtranjayroo*
forget	esquecer	*eshkessair*
fork	garfo	*garfoo*
form	impresso	*eempressoo*
fort	fortaleza	*fortalayza*
forward, send	enviar	*ainveeyar*
fountain	fonte	*font*
frame	armação	*armasow*
frank	franco	*francoo*
free	livre	*leevre*
free	gratuito	*gratooeetoo*
free time	tempo livre	*tempoo leevre*
freeze	congelar	*conjelar*
French	francês	*fransayj*
fresh	fresco	*freshcoo*
Friday	sexta-feira	*seshta fayra*
fried	frito	*freetoo*
fried egg	ovo estrelado	*ovoo shtrelardoo*
friend	amigo	*ameegoo*
friendly	simpático	*seemparteecoo*
friendly	amigavel	*ameegarvel*
fright	medo	*maydoo*
fringe	franja	*franja*
fruit	fruta	*froota*
fruit juice	sumo de frutas	*soomoo duh frootash*
frying pan	frigideira	*freejeedayra*
full	cheio	*shayoo*
fun	divertimento	*deevairteementoo*

G

gallery	galeria	*gallereea*
game	jogo	*jogoo*
garage	garagem	*gararjaim*
garden	jardim	*jardeem*
gastroenteritis	gastrenterite	*gashtrentaireet*

gauze	gaze	*gaz*
gear	velocidade	*velossidard*
gel	gel	*jel*
German	alemão	*allaymow*
get married	casar-se	*cazar-suh*
get off (e.g. a bus)	sair	*syeer*
gift	presente	*present*
gilt	dourado	*doorardoo*
ginger	gengibre	*jenjeebre*
girl	rapariga	*rapareega*
girlfriend	amiga	*ameega*
giro cheque	cheque dos correios	*sheck doosh coorayoosh*
giro guarantee card	cartão dos correios	*cartow doosj coorayoosh*
glass (for drinking)	copo	*copoo*
glass (window)	vidro	*veedroo*
glasses (sun-)	óculos (de sol)	*ocooloosh (duh sol)*
glide	planar	*plannar*
glove	luva	*loova*
glue	cola	*colla*
gnat	mosquito	*moshkeetoo*
go	ir	*ear*
go back	regressar	*regressar*
go out	sair	*syeer*
goat's cheese	queijo de cabra	*cayjoo duh cabra*
gold	ouro	*oroo*
golf course	campo de golfe	*campoo duh golf*
gone	perdido	*pairdeedoo*
good afternoon	boa tarde	*boa tard*
good evening	boa noite	*boa noyt*
good morning	bom dia	*bom deeah*
good night	boa noite	*boa noyt*
goodbye	adeus	*adayoosh*
goodbye	despedida	*deshpedeeda*
gram	grama	*grarma*
grams	gramas	*grarmash*
grandchild	neto/neta	*netoo/neta*
grandfather	avô	*avoe*

grandmother	avó	avoh
grape juice	sumo de uva	soomoo di oova
grapefruit	toranja	tooranja
grapes	uvas	oovash
grave	sepultura	sepooltoora
grease	gordura	gordoora
green	verde	vaird
green card	cartão verde	cartow vaird
greet	cumprimentar	coompreementar
grey haired	grisalho	grizalyoo
grill	grelhar	grelyar
grilled	grelhado	grelyardoo
grocer's shop	mercearia	mercyareeah
groceries	artigos de mercearia	arteegoosh duh maircyareeah
ground	chão	shau
ground beef	carne picada	carn peecarda
group	grupo	groopoo
guest house	pensão	pensow
guide (person, book)	guía	gueeah
guided tour	viagem guiada	veearjaim gueearda
gynaecologist	ginecologista	jeenaycolojeeshta

H

hair	cabelo	cabayloo
hairbrush	escova de cabelo	eshcova duh cabayloo
hairdresser	cabeleireiro, barbeiro	cabelayrayroo, barbayroo
hairpins	ganchos de cabelo	ganshoosh duh cabayloo
hairspray	laca para o cabelo	laca parra oo cabayloo
hairstyle	penteado	pentyardoo
half	meio	mayoo
half	metade	metard
half full	meio cheio	mayoo shayoo
hammer	martelo	martelloo
hand	mão	mau
handbrake	travão de mão	travow duh mau

handbag	mala	*mala*
handicrafts	artesanato	*artesanartoo*
handkerchief	lenço	*lensoo*
handmade	feito à mão	*faytoo ah mau*
happy	alegre	*allegre*
harbour	porto	*portoo*
hard	duro	*dooroo*
hat	chapéu	*shapayoo*
have dinner	jantar	*jantar*
hayfever	febre do feno	*febre doo fennoo*
hazelnut	avelã	*avelar*
head	cabeça	*cabaysa*
headache	dor de cabeça	*door duh cabaysa*
health	saúde	*sow-ood*
health food shop	loja de artigos	*loja duh arteegoosh*
	dietéticos	*dee-eteteecoosh*
hear	perceber	*pairsebbair*
hearing aid	aparelho auditivo	*aparellyoo owdeeteevoo*
heart	coração	*coorasow*
heart patient	cardíaco	*cardeeacoo*
heater	aquecimento	*akessimentoo*
heavy	pesado	*pezardoo*
heel	calcanhar	*calcanyar*
heel (shoe)	salto	*saltoo*
hello	óla	*ohla*
hello	viva	*veeva*
helmet	capacete	*cappaset*
help	ajudar	*ajoodar*
help	ajuda	*ajooda*
helping	dose	*doz*
herbal tea	chá de ervas	*shar di airvash*
herbs	ervas	*airvash*
here	aqui	*akee*
here you have	aqui tem	*akee taim*
herring	arenque	*arenk*
high	alto	*altoo*
high tide	maré cheia	*maray shaya*

highchair	cadeira de bebé	*cadayra duh baybay*
hiking	andar a pé	*andar ah peh*
hiking trip	excursão	*eshcoorsow ah peh*
hip	anca	*anca*
hire	alugar	*aloogar*
hitchhike	pedir boleia	*pedeer bolaya*
hobby	hobby	*obby*
holdup	assalto	*assaltoo*
holiday	feriado	*ferriardoo*
holiday	férias	*ferryash*
holiday house	casa de férias	*carza duh ferriash*
holiday village	aldeamento turístico	*aldayamentoo tooreeshteecoo*
homesickness	saudades	*sowdardesh*
honest	honesto	*hooneshtoo*
honey	mel	*mel*
horizontal	horizontal	*oreezontarl*
horrible	horroroso	*ororohzoo*
horse	cavalo	*cavarloo*
hospital	hospital	*oshpeetarl*
hospitality	hospitalidade	*oshpeetalidad*
hot	quente	*kent*
hotwater bottle	botija	*booteeja*
hot	picante	*peecant*
hotel	hotel	*ottel*
hour	hora	*oara*
house	casa	*carza*
household items	artigos domésticos	*arteegoosh doomeshteecoosh*
houses of parliament	edifício parlamentar	*edeefeesyoo parlamentar*
housewife	dona de casa	*donna duh carza*
how far?	a que distância?	*ah kay deeshtancia*
how long?	quanto tempo?	*cuarntoo tempoo?*
how much?	quanto?	*cuarntoo?*
how?	como?	*cohmoo?*
hurricane	ciclone	*seeeclon*

hurry	pressa	*pressa*
husband	marido	*mareedoo*
hut	cabana	*cabarna*
hyperventilation	hiperventilação	*eepairventeelasow*

I

ice cubes	cubos de gelo	*cooboosh duh jayloo*
icecream	gelado	*jelardoo*
idea	ideia	*eedaya*
identification	documento de identificação	*docoomentoo duh identeefeecasow*
identify	identificar	*eedenteefeecar*
ignition key	chave de contacto	*sharv duh contactoo*
ill	doente	*dooent*
illness	doença	*dooensa*
imagine	imaginar	*eemajeenar*
immediately	imediatamente	*eemediatament*
import duty	direito de importação	*deeraytoo di eemportasow*
impossible	impossível	*eempoosseevel*
impressions	impressões	*eempressoynsh*
in	dentro	*dentroo*
in the evening	à noitinha	*ah noyteenya*
in the morning	de manhã	*duh manyar*
included	incluído	*eenclooydoo*
included	inclusivo	*eenclooseevoo*
indicate	apontar	*appontar*
indicator	placa de sinalização	*placa duh seenaleezasow*
inexpensive	barato	*barartoo*
infection (viral/ bacterial)	infecção (virótica/ bacteriana)	*eenfecksow (veeroteeca/ bacteriana)*
inflammation	inflamação	*eenflammasow*
influenza	gripe	*greep*
information	informação	*eenformasow*
information	dados	*dardoosh*

information desk	balcão de informações	*balcow di eenformasoynsh*
injection	injecção	*eenjecksow*
injured	ferido	*ferreedoo*
inner tube	câmara de ar	*cammara di ar*
innocent	inocente	*eenoocent*
insect	insecto	*eensectoo*
insect bite	picadela de insecto	*peecadella di eensectoo*
insect repellant	repellente contra mosquitos	*repellent contra moshkeetoosh*
inside	dentro	*dentroo*
insole	palmilha	*palmeelya*
instructions	instruções	*eenshtroosoynsh*
insurance	seguro	*segooroo*
intermission	intervalo	*eentervarloo*
international	internacional	*eentairnacionarl*
interpreter	intérprete	*eentairpret*
intersection	cruzamento	*croozamentoo*
introduce oneself	apresentar-se	*aprezentar-suh*
invite	convidar	*conveedar*
iodine	iodo	*yod*
Ireland	Irlanda	*earlanda*
iron	ferro	*fehroo*
iron, to	passar a ferro	*passar ah ferroo*
iron	ferro de passar	*ferroo duh passar*
ironing board	tábua de passar	*tabooah duh passar*
island	ilha	*eelya*
Italian	italiano	*eetaliarnoo*
itch	comichão	*comeechow*

J

jack, monkey	macaco	*makarkoo*
jacket	casaco curto	*cazarcoo coortoo*
jam	doce	*dose*
January	janeiro	*janayroo*
jaw	maxilar	*maksilar*

jellyfish	alforreca	*alfoorecka*
jeweller	joalharia	*jooalyareeah*
jewellery	jóias	*joyash*
jog	fazer jogging	*fazzair joggeeng*
joke	piada	*peearda*
juice	sumo	*soomoo*
July	julho	*joolyoo*
jump leads	cabos para ligar a bateria	*carboosh parra leegar a batereeah*
jumper	camisola	*cameezola*
June	junho	*joonyoo*

K

key	chave	*sharv*
kilo	quilo	*keeloo*
kilometre	quilómetro	*keelometroo*
king	rei	*ray*
kiosk	quiosque	*keeoshk*
kiss (verb)	beijar	*bayjar*
kiss	beijo	*bayjoo*
kitchen	cozinha	*coozeenya*
knee	joelho	*jooelyoo*
knee socks	meias até o joelho	*mayash atay ow jooelyoo*
knife	faca	*facca*
knit	tricotar	*treecootar*
know	saber	*sabair*

L

lace	renda	*renda*
lace (shoe)	atacador	*attackadoor*
ladies'	lavabos de senhoras	*lavarboosh duh senyorash*
lake	lago	*largoo*
lamp	lâmpada	*lamparda*
land	terra	*terra*
lane	faixa de rodagem	*fysha duh roodarjaim*

language	língua	*leengwa*
large	grande	*grand*
last (previous)	anterior	*anterrior*
last	último	*oolteemoo*
last night	ontem à noite	*ontaim ah noyt*
late	tarde	*tard*
later, already	já	*jah*
laugh	rir	*rear*
launderette	lavandaria	*lavandareeah*
law	direito	*diraytoo*
laxative	purgativo	*poorgateevoo*
leak	furo	*fooroo*
leather	pele/couro	*pel/cooroo*
leather goods	artigos de pele	*arteegoosh duh pel*
leave	partir	*parteer*
leek	alho francês	*alyoo fransayj*
left	esquerda	*eshcairda*
left	à esquerda	*ah eshcairda*
left luggage	depósito de bagagem	*depozzeetoo duh bagarjaim*
leg	perna	*pairna*
lemon	limão	*leemow*
lend	emprestar	*aimpreshtar*
lens	lente	*lent*
lentils	lentilhas	*lenteelyash*
less	menos	*menoosh*
lesson	lição	*leesow*
letter	carta	*carta*
lettuce	alface	*alfass*
level crossing	passagem de nível	*passarjaim duh neevel*
library	biblioteca	*beebleeootehca*
lie	mentir	*menteer*
lie	deitarse	*daytarse*
lift (hitchhike)	boleia	*boolaya*
lift (in building)	elevador	*eelevadoor*
light (not dark)	claro	*claroo*
light (not heavy)	leve	*lev*

light	luz	*loosh*
light, to	acender	*assendair*
lighter	isqueiro	*eeshkayroo*
lighthouse	farol	*farol*
lightning	raio	*ryoo*
like	gostar de	*goshtar duh*
line	linha	*leenya*
linen	linho	*leenyoo*
lipstick	batôn	*baton*
liqueur	licor	*leecor*
liquorice	alcaçuz	*alcasooj*
listen	ouvir	*ohveer*
literature	literatura	*leeteratoora*
litre	litro	*leetroo*
little	pouco	*pohcoo*
live	morar	*moorar*
live together	viver junto	*veevair joontoo*
lobster	lagosta	*lagoshta*
local	local	*loocal*
lock	fechadura	*feshadoora*
long	comprido	*compreedoo*
long lasting	de longa duração	*duh longa doorasow*
look	olhar	*oolyar*
look for	procurar	*procoorar*
lorry	camião	*cammyow*
lose	perder	*pairdair*
loss	perda	*pairda*
lost	perdido	*pairdeedoo*
lost property office	achados e perdidos	*ashardoosh ee perdeedooz*
lotion	loção	*loosow*
loud	alto	*altoo*
love, to	gostar/amar	*goshtar/amar*
love	amor	*amor*
low	baixo	*byshoo*
low tide	maré baixa	*maray bysha*
luck	sorte	*sort*

luggage	bagagem	*bagarjaim*
luggage locker	cofre de bagagem	*cofre duh bagarjaim*
lunch	almoço	*almoesoo*
lungs	pulmões	*poolmoynsh*

M

macaroni	macarrão	*macarrow*
machine (vending)	vendedor automático	*vendador owtoomateecoo*
madam	senhora	*senyora*
magazine	revista	*reveeshta*
mail	correio	*coorayoo*
main post office	correio central	*coorayoo centrarl*
main road	estrada	*eshtrarda*
make an appointment	marcar um encontro	*marcar oom aincontroo*
make love	fazer amor	*fazzair amor*
makeshift	provisório	*prooveesoryoo*
man	homem	*omaim*
manager	gerente	*jerrent*
mandarin	tangerina	*tanjereena*
manicure	manicure	*manicure*
map	mapa	*mapa*
marble	mármore	*marmora*
March	março	*marsoo*
margarine	margarina	*margareena*
marina	marina	*mareena*
market	mercado	*mercardoo*
marriage, wedding	casamento	*cazamento*
married	casado	*cazardoo*
mass	missa	*meessa*
massage	massagem	*massarjaim*
matt	sem brilho	*saim breelyoo*
match	desafio/jogo	*dezafyoo/jogoo*
matches	fósforos	*foshforoosh*
May	maio	*myoo*

maybe	talvez	*talvayj*
mayonnaise	maionese	*myonez*
mayor	presidente da câmara/prefeito	*prezeedent da cammara/preffaytoo*
meal	refeição	*refaysow*
mean	significar	*seegneefeecar*
meat	carne	*carn*
medication, medicine	medicamento/ remédio	*medicamentoo/ remedyoo*
meet	conhecer	*coonyessair*
melon	melão	*melow*
membership	adesão	*adezow*
menstruate	menstruar	*menshtrooar*
menstruation	menstruação	*menshtruasow*
menu	menu, ementa	*menoo, ementa*
menu of the day	menu do dia	*menoo doo dia*
message	mensagem	*mensarjaim*
metal	metal	*mettal*
meter	taxímetro	*tackseemetroo*
metre	metro	*metroo*
migraine	enxaqueca	*ainshakeka*
milk	leite	*layt*
millimetre	milímetro	*meeleemetroo*
milometer	contaquilómetros	*conta keelometroosh*
mineral water	água mineral	*agwa meeneral*
minute	minuto	*meenootoo*
mirror	espelho	*shpelyoo*
miss	sentir a falta	*senteer ah falta*
missing person	desaparecido	*dezaparesseedoo*
mistake	erro	*ehroo*
mistake	engano	*aingarnoo*
misunderstanding	malentendido	*mal entendeedoo*
mixture	mistura	*meeshtoora*
modern art	arte moderna	*art mooderna*
molar	molar	*moolar*
moment	um momento	*oom momentoo*
monastery	mosteiro	*mooshtayroo*

Monday	segunda-feira	*segoonda fayra*
money	dinheiro	*deenyayroo*
month	mês	*mayj*
moped	bicicleta motorizada	*beeceecletta mottooreezarda*
more and more	cada vez mais	*cadda vaij mysh*
morning-after pill	pílula `morning after'	*peeloola `morning-after'*
mosque	mesquita	*meshkeeta*
motel	motel	*mohtel*
mother	mãe	*my*
motor cross	motociclismo	*motooseecleejmoo*
motorbike	motocicleta	*motooseeclayta*
motorboat	barco a motor	*barcoo ah motor*
motorway	autoestrada	*owtooshtrarda*
mountain	monte	*mont*
mountain hut	refúgio	*refoogyoo*
mountaineering	alpinismo	*alpeeneejmoo*
mountaineering shoes	sapatos de alpinismo	*sapartoosh duh alpeeneejmoo*
mouse	rato	*rartoo*
mouth	boca	*boca*
much/many	muito/muitos	*mweentoo/mweentoosh*
multi-storey car park	parque de vários andares	*park duh varyooz andaresh*
muscle	músculo	*mooshcooloo*
muscle spasms	cãibras	*kybraj*
museum	museu	*moosayoo*
mushrooms	cogumelos	*cogoomeloosh*
music	música	*mooseeca*
musical	musical	*mooseecal*
mussels	mexilhões	*mesheelyoynsh*
mustard	mostarda	*mooshtarda*

N

nail	unha	*oonya*
nail (metal)	prego	*praygoo*

nail polish	verniz para as unhas	*verneej parra az oonyash*
nail polish remover	acetona para as unhas	*assaytona parra az oonyash*
nail scissors	tesoura de unhas	*tezora di oonyash*
naked	nu	*noo*
nappy	fralda	*fralda*
nationality	nacionalidade	*nasionaleedad*
natural	naturalmente	*natooralment*
nature	natureza	*natoorayza*
naturism	naturismo	*natooreejmoo*
naturist beach	praia de naturistas	*prya duh natooreeshtash*
nauseous	enjoativo	*ainjooateevoo*
near	perto de	*pairtoo duh*
nearby	perto	*pairtoo*
necessary	necessário	*necessaryoo*
neck	pescoço	*peshcossoo*
necklace	fio	*feeoo*
nectarine	nectarina	*nectareena*
needle	agulha	*agoolya*
negative	negativo	*negateevoo*
neighbours	vizinhos	*veezeenyoosh*
nephew	sobrinho	*soobreenyoo*
never	nunca	*noonca*
new	novo	*nohvoo*
news	notícias	*nooteeciash*
newspaper	jornal	*jornal*
next	seguinte	*segeent*
next to	ao lado	*ow lardoo*
nice (friendly)	simpático	*seemparteecoo*
nice (to taste)	agradável, bonito	*agradarvel, booneetoo*
niece	sobrinha	*soobreenya*
night	noite	*noyt*
night duty	serviço nocturno	*sairveesoo noctoornoo*
nightclub	clube nocturno	*cloob noctoornoo*
nightlife	vida nocturna	*veeda noctoorna*
no one	ninguém	*neengaim*
no	não	*now*

no overtaking	proibido de ultrapassar	*prooeebeedoo duh ooltrapassar*
noise	barulho	*baroolyoo*
nonstop	directo (sem paragens)	*deerectoo (saim pararjainsh)*
normal	normal	*normal*
north	norte	*nort*
nose	nariz	*nareej*
nose drops	gotas para o nariz	*gotash parra oo nareej*
notepaper	papel de escrever	*papel duh eshcrevair*
nothing	nada	*narda*
November	novembro	*noovembroo*
nowhere	em parte nenhuma	*aim part nenyooma*
number	número	*noomeroo*
number plate	matrícula	*matreecoola*
nurse	enfermeira	*ainfairmayra*
nutmeg	noz moscada	*noj mooshcarda*
nuts (mixed)	nozes (mistura)	*nozesh (meeshtoora)*

O

October	outubro	*ohtoobroo*
offer	oferecer	*ofressair*
office	escritório	*eshcreetoryoo*
oil	óleo	*ollyoo*
oil level	nível do óleo	*neevel doo ollyoo*
ointment	pomada	*poomarda*
ointment for burns	pomada contra queimaduras	*poomarda contra kaymadurash*
okay	de acordo	*di acordoo*
old	velho	*velyoo*
olive oil	azeite	*azayt*
olives	azeitonas	*azaytonash*
omelette	omeleta	*omelayta*
on	em cima de	*aim seema duh*
on board	a bordo	*ah bordoo*
on the right	direito	*diraytoo*

on the way	no caminho	*noo cameenyoo*
oncoming car	em sentido contrário	*aim senteedoo contraryoo*
oneway traffic	trânsito de sentido único	*transeetoo duh senteedoo ooneecoo*
onion	cebola	*sebolla*
open	aberto	*abairtoo*
open	abrir	*abreer*
opera	ópera	*opera*
operate	operar	*operar*
operator (telephone)	telefonista	*telefoneeshta*
operetta	opereta	*operetta*
opposite	em frente	*aim frent*
optician	oculista	*occooleeshta*
orange (colour)	cor de laranja	*coor duh laranja*
orange	laranja	*laranja*
orange juice	sumo de laranja	*soomoo duh laranja*
order (in -,) tidy	em ordem	*aim ordaim*
order	encomenda	*aincoomenda*
order, to	encomendar	*aincoomendar*
other	outro	*ohtroo*
other side	do outro lado	*doo ohtroo lardoo*
outside	fora	*forra*
overtake	ultrapassar	*ooltrapassar*
oysters	ostras	*oshtrash*

P

packed lunch	merenda/lanche	*merenda/lansh*
packet (of cigarettes)	pacote (de cigarros)	*packot (duh seegarroosh)*
page	página	*parjeena*
pain	dor	*door*
painkiller	analgésico	*analjezeecoo*
paint	tinta	*teenta*
painting	pintura	*peentoora*
palace	palácio	*palassio*

pan	panela	*panella*
pancake	crepe	*crep*
pane	vidro	*veedroo*
pants, briefs, knickers	cuecas	*cooeckash*
panty liner	penso de protecção	*pensoo duh prootecsow*
paper	papel	*papel*
paprika	pimento	*peementoo*
paraffin oil	petróleo	*petrollyoo*
parasol	chapéu de sol	*shapayoo duh sol*
parcel	encomenda postal	*aimcoomenda pooshtal*
parcel	pacote	*packot*
pardon	desculpe	*deshcoolp*
parents	pais	*pysh*
park	parque	*park*
park	estacionar	*estassionar*
parking space	lugar para estacionar	*loogar parra eshtassionar*
parsley	salsa	*salsa*
part (car)	peça	*pessa*
partition	separação	*separação*
partner	companheiro	*companyayroo*
party	festa	*feshta*
passable (road)	transitável	*transeetarvel*
passenger	passageiro	*passajayroo*
passport	passaporte	*passaport*
passport photo	foto tipo passe	*fotoo teepoo pass*
patient	doente	*dooent*
pavement	passeio/calçada	*passayoo/calsarda*
pay	pagar	*paggar*
pay the bill	pagar a conta	*pagar a conta*
peach	pêssego	*pessaygoo*
peanuts	amendoins	*amendooeensh*
pear	pera	*paira*
peas	ervilhas	*airveelyash*
pedal	pedalo	*pedarloo*
pedestrian crossing	passagem para peões	*passarjaim parra peeoynsh*

pedicure	pedicure	*pedicure*
pen	caneta	*canetta*
pencil (hard/soft)	lápis (duro/macio)	*larpeej (dooroo/maseeyoo)*
penis	pénis	*penneej*
penknife	canivete	*canivet*
pepper	pimenta	*peementa*
performance (show)	representação	*representasow*
perfume	perfume	*perfoom*
perm	permanente	*permanent*
perm, to have a...	fazer uma permanente	*fazzair ooma permanent*
permit	licença	*leesensa*
person	pessoa	*pessoa*
personal	pessoal	*pessoal*
petrol	gasolina	*gazooleena*
petrol station	estação de serviço/ posto de gasolina	*eshtasow duh serveesoo/ poshtoo duh gazooleena*
pets	animais de estimação	*animysh duh eshteemasow*
pharmacy	farmácia	*farmassia*
phone (tele-)	telefone	*telefon*
phone (verb)	telefonar	*telefoonar*
phone box	cabine telefónica	*cabeen telefoneeca*
phone directory	lista telefónica	*leeshta telefoneeca*
phone number	número de telefone	*noomeroo duh telefon*
photo	fotografia	*fotografeea*
photocopier	máquina copiadora	*markeena copiadoora*
photocopy (verb)	fotocopiar	*fotoocoopiar*
photocopy	fotocópia	*fotoocopia*
pick up	ir buscar	*ear booshcar*
picnic	piquenique	*peekneek*
piece of clothing	peça de roupa	*pessa duh roepa*
pier	pontão/cais	*pontow/kysh*
pigeon	pombo	*pomboo*
pill (contraceptive)	pílula anticoncepcional	*peeloola anticonsepcional*

pillow	almofada	*almoofarda*
pillowcase	fronha	*fronya*
pin	alfinete	*alfeenet*
pineapple	ananás	*ananash*
pipe	cachimbo	*casheemboo*
pipe tobacco	tabaco para cachimbo	*tabacoo parra casheemboo*
pity	(ter) pena	*(tair) penna*
place of interest	lugares turísticos	*loogaresh tooreeshteecoosh*
plan	planta	*planta*
plant	planta	*planta*
plasters	pensos	*pensoosh*
plastic	plástico	*plashteecoo*
plate, dish, course	prato	*prartoo*
platform	linha	*leenya*
platform	cais	*kysh*
play, (theatre)	peça de teatro	*pessa duh teeartroo*
play	brincar	*breencar*
play basketball	jogar basquetebol	*joogar bashketboll*
play draughts	jogar às damas	*joogar as damash*
play golf	jogar golfe	*joogar golf*
play tennis	jogar ténis	*joogar teneej*
playground	jardim infantil	*jardeem eenfanteel*
playing cards	cartas de jogar	*cartash duh joogar*
pleasant	agradável	*agradarvel*
please	se faz favor	*suh faj favvor*
pleasure	prazer	*prazzair*
plum	ameixa	*amaysha*
point	indicar	*eendeecar*
poison	veneno	*venenoo*
police	polícia	*poleesia*
police station	posto da polícia	*poshtoo da poleesia*
police officer	polícia	*poleesia*
pond	tanque	*tank*
pony	pónei	*pohnay*
pop concert	concerto de pop	*consairtoo duh pop*

population	população	*poopoolasow*
pork	carne de porco	*carn duh porcoo*
port-wine	vinho do Porto	*veenyoo doo portoo*
porter	bagageiro	*bagajayroo*
porter	porteiro	*portayroo*
post code	código postal	*codeegoo pooshtal*
post office	agência do correio	*ajencia do coorayoo*
postage	porte	*port*
postbox	caixa de correio	*kysha duh coorayoo*
postcard	postal	*pooshtal*
postman	carteiro	*cartayroo*
potato	batata	*batarta*
poultry	aves	*arvesh*
pound	libra	*leebra*
powdered milk	leite em pó	*layt aim poh*
power point	ligação eléctrica/	*leegasow eeletreeca/*
	tomada	*toomarda*
pram	carrinho de bébé	*carreenyoo duh baybay*
prawns	camarões	*cammaroynsh*
precious	precioso	*pressiozoo*
prefer, to	preferir	*prefereer*
preference	preferência	*preferensia*
pregnant	grávida	*graveeda*
present	presente	*prezzent*
pressure	stress	*shtress*
price	preço	*praysoo*
price list	lista de preços	*leeshta duh praysoosh*
print	imprimir	*eempreemeer*
print (verb)	fazer cópias	*fazair coppyash*
print	cópia	*cohpya*
probably	provavelmente	*proovarvelment*
problem	problema	*prooblayma*
profession	profissão	*proofeesow*
programme	programa	*proograma*
pronounce	pronunciar	*proonunciar*
propane/butane	gás de campismo	*gaj duh campeejmoo*
(camping gas)	(propano/butano)	*(proparnoo/bootarnoo)*

provident fund	caixa de previdência	*kysha duh preveedencia*
prune	ameixa seca	*amaysha seca*
pudding	pudim	*poodeem*
pull (tooth)	tirar (dente)	*teerar (dent)*
pull a muscle	distender um	*deeshtendair oom*
	músculo	*mooshcooloo*
pure	puro	*pooroo*
purple	violeta	*veeooleta*
purse	portamoedas	*porta mooaydash*
push	empurrar	*aimpurrar*
puzzle	puzzle	*puzzel*
pyjamas	pijama	*peejama*

Q

quarter	quarto	*cwartoo*
quarter of an hour	quarto de hora	*cwartoo duh ora*
queen	rainha	*ryeenya*
question	pergunta	*pairgoonta*
quick	rápido	*rapeedoo*
quiet	calmo	*calmoo*

R

radio	rádio	*rardyoo*
railways	caminhos de ferro	*cameenyoosh duh feroo*
rain	chuva	*shoova*
rain, to	chover	*choovair*
raincoat	impermeável	*eempairmeearvel*
raisins	passas	*passash*
rape	violação	*veeolasow*
rapids	cachoeiro	*cashooayroo*
raspberries	framboesas	*frambooayzash*
raw	cru	*croo*
raw vegetables	legumes crus	*legoomesh croosh*
razor blades	giletes	*geeletsch*
read	ler	*lair*

ready	pronto	*prontoo*
receipt	talão, recibo	*tallow, resseeboo*
recipe	receita	*resayta*
reclining chair	cadeira-cama	*cadayra camma*
recommend	recomendar	*recoomendar*
rectangle	rectângulo	*retangooloo*
red	encarnado/vermelho	*encarnardoo/vermelyoo*
red wine	vinho tinto	*veenyoo teentoo*
reduction	desconto	*deshcontoo*
refrigerator	frigorífico	*freegoreefeecoo*
regards	cumprimentos	*coompreementoosh*
region	região	*rejiow*
registered	registado	*rejeeshtardo*
registration document	livrete	*leevret*
relatives	família	*fameelia*
reliable	confiável	*confeearvel*
religion	religião	*releegeeow*
rent out	alugar	*aloogar*
repair	reparar/concertar	*reparar/consairtar*
repairs	reparações/ consertos	*reparasoynsh/ consairtoosh*
repeat	repetir	*repeteer*
report	relatório	*relatoryoo*
resent	levar a mal	*levar ah mal*
responsible	responsável	*responsarvel*
rest	descansar	*deshcansar*
restaurant	restaurante	*reshtowrant*
result	resultado	*resooltardoo*
retired	reformado	*reformardoo*
return (ticket)	ida e volta (bilhete)	*eeda ee vollta (beelyet)*
reverse (vehicle)	fazer marcha atrás	*fazair marsha atraj*
rheumatism	reumatismo	*rayoomateesjmoo*
rice	arroz	*arroj*
ridiculous	estúpido/ridículo	*eshtoopeedoo/ reedeecooloo*
riding (horseback)	andar a cavalo	*andar ah cavarloo*

riding school	picadeiro	*peecadayroo*
right	para a direita	*parra ah dirayta*
right of way	prioridade	*preeorridard*
ripe	maduro	*madooroo*
risk	risco	*reeshcoo*
river	rio	*reeoo*
road	rua	*rooah*
roadway	estrada	*estrarda*
roasted	assado	*assardoo*
rock	rocha	*rosha*
roll	pãozinho	*powzeenyoo*
	(sem manteiga)	*(saim mantayga)*
rolling tobacco	cigarro de enrolar	*seegarroo di ainroolar*
roof rack	portabagagem	*porta bagarjaim*
room	quarto	*cwartoo*
room number	número do quarto	*noomeroo doo cwartoo*
room service	serviço de quarto	*sairveesoo duh cwartoo*
rope	cordel/corda	*cordel/corda*
rosé	rosé	*rozay*
roundabout	rotunda	*rotoonda*
route	caminho	*cameenyoo*
rowing boat	barco à remos	*barcoo ah remoosh*
rubber	borracha	*borasha*
rubbish	lixo	*leeshoo*
rubbish bag	saco do lixo	*sarcoo duh leeshoo*
rubbish, nonsense	estupidez	*eshtoopeedej*
rucksack	mochila	*mosheela*
rude	malcriado	*malcreeardo*
ruins	ruínas	*roo-eenash*
run into	encontrar	*aincontrar*

S

sad	triste	*treesht*
safari	safari	*safaree*
safe	seguro	*segooroo*
safe	cofre	*cofre*

safety pin	alfinete de segurança	*alfeenet duh segooransa*
sail	velejar	*velejar*
sailing boat	barco à vela	*barcoo ah vella*
salad	salada	*salarda*
salad oil	óleo para salada	*ollyoo parra salarda*
salami	salame	*salam*
sale	saldo/liquidação	*saldoo/leekeedasow*
salt	sal	*sal*
same	mesmo	*mejmoo*
sandy beach	praia de areia	*prya duh arraya*
sanitary pad	penso higiénico	*pensoo eegeneecoo*
sardines	sardinhas	*sardeenyash*
satisfied	satisfeito	*sateeshfaytoo*
Saturday	sábado	*sarbadoo*
sauce	molho	*molyoo*
sauna	sauna	*sowna*
sausage (preserved)	chouriço	*shooreesoo*
savoury	salgado	*salgardoo*
say	dizer	*deezair*
scarf	cachecol	*cashcol*
scenic walk	percurso turístico	*paircoorsoo tooreeshteecoo*
school	escola	*shcola*
scissors	tesoura	*tezora*
scooter	scooter	*scootair*
scorpion	escorpião	*eshcorpyow*
Scotland	Escócia	*eshcossia*
scrambled eggs	ovos mexidos	*ovoosh mesheedoosh*
screw	parafuso	*parrafoozoo*
screwdriver	chave de fenda	*sharv duh fenda*
sculpture	escultura	*eshcooltoora*
sea	mar	*mar*
seasick	enjoado	*ainjoooardoo*
seat	lugar sentado	*loogar sentardoo*
secondhand	segunda mão	*segoonda mau*
second	segundo	*segoondoo*

sedative	sedativo	*sedateevoo*
see, visit	visitar	*veezeetar*
send	enviar	*ainvyar*
sentence	frase	*fraz*
September	setembro	*setembroo*
serious, grave	grave	*grarv*
serious, responsible	sério	*sairyoo*
service	serviço	*serveesoo*
serviette	guardanapo	*gwardanarpoo*
sewing thread	linhas de costura	*leenyash duh coshtoora*
shade	sombra	*sombra*
shallow	pouco fundo	*pohcoo foondoo*
shammy	camurça	*camoorsa*
shampoo	champô	*shampoh*
shark	tubarão	*toobarow*
shave	barbear	*barbyar*
shaver	máquina de barbear	*markeena duh barbyar*
shaving brush	pincel de barba	*peensel duh barba*
shaving cream	creme de barbear	*crem duh barbyar*
shaving soap	sabão de barbear	*sabow duh barbyar*
sheet	lençol	*lensol*
sherry	xerez	*sherayj*
shirt	camisa	*cameeza*
shoe	sapato	*sapartoo*
shoe polish	pomada de engraixar	*poomarda di aingryshar*
shoe shop	sapataria	*sapattareeah*
shoemaker	sapateiro	*sappatayroo*
shop	loja	*loja*
shop assistant	empregada	*aimpregarda*
shop window	montra	*montra*
shopping	fazer compras	*fazzair comprash*
shopping centre	centro comercial	*sentroo coomerciarl*
short	curto	*coortoo*
short circuit	curtocircuito	*coortoo seercooeetoo*
shorts	calças curtas	*calsash coortash*
shoulder	ombro	*ombroo*
show	espectáculo	*eshpetarcooloo*

shower	duche	doosh
shutter (camera)	diafragma	deeafragma
sieve	peneira	penayra
sign	painel/sinal	pynel/seenal
sign	assinar	asseenar
signature	assinatura	assenatoora
silence	silêncio	seelensyoo
silver	prata	prarta
silverplated	prateado	pratyardoo
simple	simples	seemplesh
single	solteiro	soltayroo
single	individual	eendeeveedual
single ticket	bilhete de ida	beelyet duh eeda
sir	senhor	senyor
sister	irmã	eermar
sit	sentar-se	sentar-suh
size	número	noomeroo
size	tamanho	tamanyoo
skate	patinar	pateenar
skimmed	meio gordo	mayoo gordoo
skin	pele	pel
skirt	saia	syah
sleep	dormir	doormeer
sleeping car	carruagem cama	carruarjaim camma
sleeping pills	comprimidos para dormir	compreemeedoosh parra doormeer
slide	diapositivo	deeapozeeteevoo
slip road	entrada para a rodovia	entrarda parra ah rodooveeah
slow	devagar	deevagar
slow train	comboio ronceiro	comboyoo ronsayroo
small	pequeno	peekenoo
small change	dinheiro trocado, troco	deenyayroo troocardoo, trocoo
smell, to	cheirar mal	shayrar mal
smoke	fumo	foomoo
smoke	fumar	foomar

take	tomar	*toomar*
take, last	durar	*durar*
taken, engaged	ocupado	*occoopardoo*
talcum powder	(pó de) talco	*(poh duh) talcoo*
talk	falar	*falar*
tall	alto	*altoo*
tampons	tampões	*tampoynsh*
tanned	bronzeado	*bronzyardoo*
tap	torneira	*tornayra*
tap water	água da torneira	*agwa da tornayra*
taste	provar	*proovar*
taxi	táxi	*tarksy*
taxi rank	praça de táxis	*prassa duh tarkseesh*
tea	chá	*shar*
teapot	bule	*bool*
teaspoon	colher de chá	*coolyair duh shar*
telegram	telegrama	*telegrarma*
telephoto lens	teleobjectiva	*tele objeteeva*
television	televisão	*televeesow*
telex	telex	*telex*
temperature (weather)	temperatura	*temperatoora*
temporary filling	obturação temporária	*obtoorasow temporaria*
tender	tenro	*tenroo*
tennis ball	bola de ténis	*bola duh teneej*
tennis court	campo de ténis	*campoo duh teneej*
tennis racket	raquete de ténis	*raket duh teneej*
tenpin bowling	jogar bowling	*joogar bowling*
tent	tenda	*tenda*
tent peg	espia/estaca	*eshpeea/eshtarca*
terrace	esplanada	*eshplanarda*
terribly	terrivelment	*terreevelment*
thank	agradecer	*agradaysair*
thank you	muito obrigado	*mweentoo obrigardoo*
thanks	obrigado	*obrigardoo*

the day after tomorrow	depois de amanhã	*depoysh di amanyar*
theatre	teatro	*teeartroo*
theft	roubo	*roeboo*
there	ali	*alee*
thermal bath	banho termal	*barnyoo termal*
thermometer	termómetro	*termometroo*
thick	espesso	*eshpessoo*
thief	ladrão	*ladrow*
thigh	coxa	*cosha*
thin	fino	*feenoo*
thin	magro	*magroo*
things	coisas	*coyzash*
think	pensar	*pensar*
third	terço/terceiro	*tairsoo/tairsayroo*
thirsty, to be	ter (estar com) sede	*tair (eshtar com) sed*
this afternoon	esta tarde	*eshta tard*
this evening, tonight	esta noite	*eshta noyt*
this morning	esta manhã	*eshta manyar*
thread	fiozinho/linha	*feeyoozeenyoo/leenya*
throat	garganta	*garganta*
throat lozenges	pastilhas para a garganta	*pashteelyash parra a garganta*
thunderstorm	trovoada	*troovooarda*
Thursday	quinta-feira	*keenta fayra*
ticket	bilhete	*beelyet*
ticket window, bank counter	guiché	*gueeshay*
tickets	bilhetes	*beelyetsch*
tidy	arrumar	*arroomar*
tie	gravata	*gravarta*
tights	collants	*collan*
time	tempo	*tempoo*
timer	timer	*timer*
timetable	horário	*oraryoo*
tin	lata	*larta*
tip	gorjeta	*gorjeta*

tissues	lenços de papel	*lensoosh duh papel*
toast (drink)	brinde	*breend*
toast (bread)	torrada/tosta	*toorarda/toshta*
tobacco	tabaco	*tabarcoo*
today	hoje	*oarge*
toe	dedo do pé	*daydoo doo peh*
together	juntos	*joontoosh*
toilet	lavabos	*lavarboosh*
toilet paper	papel higiénico	*papel eegeneecoo*
toiletries	artigos de toilete	*arteegoosh duh twalet*
tomato	tomate	*toomat*
tomato purée	puré de tomate	*pooray duh toomat*
tomato sauce	ketchup	*keshoop*
tomorrow	amanhã	*amarnyar*
tongue	língua	*leengwa*
tonic water	água tónica	*agwa toneeca*
too much	demais	*demysh*
tools	ferramenta	*ferramenta*
tooth	dente	*dent*
toothache	dor de dentes	*door duh dentsh*
toothbrush	escova de dentes	*eshcova duh dentsh*
toothpaste	pasta de dentes	*pashta duh dentsh*
toothpick	palito	*paleetoo*
top up	encher	*ainshair*
total	total	*tootal*
tough	duro	*dooroo*
tour	passeio (turístico)	*passayoo (tooreeshteecoo)*
tour guide	guía turístico	*gueeah tooreeshteeco*
tourist class	classe turística	*class tooreeshteeca*
Tourist Information office	agência de turismo	*ajencia duh tooreejmoo*
tourist menu	ementa turística	*ementa tooreeshteeca*
tourist ticket	bilhete turístico	*beelyet tooreeshteeco*
tow, to	rebocar	*reboocar*
towel	toalha	*tooalya*
tower	torre	*torr*

towing cable	cabo para rebocar	carboo parra reboocar
town	cidade	sidarde
town hall	câmara municipal	carmara mooneeceepal
toys	brinquedo	breenkaydoo
traffic	trânsito	transeetoo
traffic light	semáforo	semafforoo
train	comboio	comboyoo
train ticket	bilhete de combóio	beelyet duh comboyoo
train timetable	horário de combóio	oraryoo duh comboyoo
trainers	tênis	teneej
translate	traduzir	tradoozeer
travel	viajar	veeajar
travel agent	agência de viagens	ajencia duh veearjainsh
travel guide	guia	gueeah
traveller	viajante	veeajant
traveller's cheque	traveller cheque	traveller sheck
treacle/syrup	xarope	sharop
treatment	tratamento	tratamentoo
triangle	triângulo	treeangooloo
trim (hair)	aparar	apparrar
trip	passeio	passayoo
trip	excursão	eshcoorsow
trip	viagem	veearjaim
trip	voltinha	volteenya
trouble	dor	door
trout	truta	troota
trunk call	chamada interurbana	shamarda eenteroorbarna
trustworthy person	pessoa de confiança	pessoa duh confeeansa
try on	provar	proovar
tube	bisnaga	beejnarga
Tuesday	terça-feira	tairsa fayra
tumble drier	máquina de secar	markeena duh seccar
tuna	atum	atoom
tunnel	túnel	toonel
turn	turno	toornoo
TV	TV	tayvay

TV guide	guia de TV	*gueeah duh tayvay*
tweezers	pinça	*peensa*
tyre	pneu	*pnayoo*
tyre lever	desmontador	*dejmontador*
tyre pressure	pressão dos pneus	*pressow doosh penayoosh*

U

ugly	feio	*fayoo*
umbrella	chapéu de chuva	*shapayoo duh shoova*
under	em baixo	*aim byshoo*
underground	metropolitano	*metroopooleetarnoo*
underground railway system	rede de metropolitano	*red duh metroopooleetarnoo*
underground station	estação de metropolitano	*eshtasow duh metroopooleetarnoo*
understand	compreender	*compree-endair*
underwear	roupa interior	*roepa eenterrior*
undress	despir	*despeer*
unemployed	desempregado	*dezaimpregardoo*
uneven	acidentado	*assdentardoo*
university	universidade	*ooniversidarde*
unleaded	sem chumbo	*saim shoomboo*
urgent	urgente	*oorgent*
urgently	urgentemente	*oorgentment*
urine	urina	*ooreena*
usually	geralmente	*gerarlment*

V

vacate	desocupar	*dezocoopar*
vaccinate	vacinar	*vasseenar*
vagina	vagina	*vajeena*
vaginal infection	infecção vaginal	*eenfecksow vajeenal*
valid	válido	*valleedoo*
valley	vale	*val*

valuable	valioso	*vallyoezoo*
van	carrinha	*careenya*
vanilla	baunilha	*bowneelya*
vase	jarra	*jahra*
vaseline	vaselina	*vasseleena*
veal	carne de vitela	*carn duh veetela*
vegetable soup	sopa de legumes	*soppa duh legoomesh*
vegetables	legumes	*legoomesh*
vegetarian	vegetariano	*vejetaryarnoo*
vein	veia	*veya*
venereal disease	doença venérea	*dooensa venerria*
via	através de	*atravej duh*
video camera	cámara de vídeo	*camara duh veedyoo*
video recorder	gravador de vídeo	*gravvadoor duh veedyoo*
video tape	cassette de vídeo	*casset duh veedyoo*
view	vista	*veeshta*
village	aldeia	*aldaya*
visa	visto	*veeshtoo*
visit	visita	*vizeeta*
vitamin tablets	vitaminas em comprimido	*veetameenash aim compreemeedoo*
vitamin	vitamina	*veetameena*
volcano	vulcão	*voolcow*
volleyball, to play	jogar voleibol	*joogar volaybol*
vomit	vomitar	*voomeetar*

W

wait	esperar	*eshperar*
waiter	empregado/garçom	*empregardoo/garsoom*
waiting room	sala de espera	*sarla di eshpaira*
waitress	empregada	*empregarda*
wake up	despertar	*deshpairtar*
Wales	Gales	*garlesh*
walk	passeio	*passayoo*
walk	passear	*passayar*
walk	andar	*andar*

wallet	carteira	*cartayra*
wardrobe	guardaroupa	*gwarda roepa*
warm, heat	calor	*calor*
warn	avisar	*aveezar*
warning	aviso	*aveezoo*
wash	lavar	*lavar*
washing	roupa	*roepa*
washing line	corda de estender roupa	*corda di eshtendair roepa*
washing machine	máquina de lavar	*markeena duh lavar*
washing powder	sabão em pó	*sabow aim poh*
wasp	vespa	*veshpa*
watch, clock	relógio	*relogyoo*
water	água	*agwa*
waterfall	queda d'água	*kayda di agwa*
water ski	esqui aquático	*eshkee akwateecoo*
waterproof	impermeável	*eempairmeearvel*
wavepool	jacuzzi	*jacoozi*
way	lado/direcção	*lardoo (deeressow)*
we	nós	*noj*
weak	fraco	*frarcoo*
weather	tempo	*tempoo*
weather forecast	boletim meteorológico	*boleteem metrolojeecoo*
wedding	casamento	*cazzamentoo*
Wednesday	quarta-feira	*cwarta fayra*
week	semana	*semarna*
weekend	fim de semana	*feem duh semarna*
weekend duty	serviço de fim de semana	*sairveesoo duh feem duh semarna*
weekly ticket	passe semanal	*pass semarnal*
welcome	bem vindo	*baim veendoo*
well cooked	bem passado	*baim passardoo*
well, good	bom/bem	*bom/baim*
west	oeste	*wesht*
wet	húmido	*oomeedoo*
wet (weather)	chuvoso	*shoovozoo*

wetsuit	fato de surfe	fartoo duh surf
what?	o quê?	oo kay?
wheel	roda	rodda
wheelchair	cadeira de rodas	cadayra duh roddash
when?	quando?	cwarndoo
where?	onde?	ond
which?	qual?	cwarl
whipped cream	chantilly	shanteelee
white	branco	brancoo
white kidney beans	feijão branco	fayjow brancoo
who?	quem?	kaim
wholemeal	integral	eentegral
wholemeal bread	pão integral	pow eentegral
why?	porquê?	porkay?
wide-angle lens	objectiva de grande abertura	objeteeva duh grand abairtoora
widow	viúva	veeoova
widower	viúvo	veeoovoo
wife	mulher/esposa	moolyair/eshpoza
wind	vento	ventoo
windbreak	páravento	parra ventoo
windmill	moinho	mooeenyoo
window	janela	janella
windscreen wiper	limpa pára-brisas	leempa parra-breezash
wine	vinho	veenyoo
wine list	lista de vinhos	leeshta duh veenyoosh
wine shop	casa de vinhos	carza duh veenyoosh
winter	inverno	eenvairnoo
witness	testemunha	teshtemoonya
woman	mulher	moolyair
wood	madeira	madayra
wool	lã	lar
word	palavra	palavra
work	trabalho	trabalyoo
working day	dia útil	deeah ooteel
worn	usado	oosardoo
worried	preocupado	preeoccupardoo

wound	ferida	*fereeda*
wrap	embrulhar	*aimbroolyar*
wrist	pulso	*poolsoo*
write	escrever	*eshcrevair*
writing pad	bloco	*blohkoo*
(squared, lined)	(quadrado, pautado)	*(qwardrardoo, powtardoo)*
written	por escrito	*por shcreetoo*
wrong	errado	*errardoo*

Y

yacht	iate	*yat*
year	ano	*arnoo*
yellow	amarelo	*amarelloo*
yes	sim	*si*
yes, please	sim, se faz favor	*si, suh faj favvor*
yesterday	ontem	*ontaim*
yoghurt	iogurte	*yogoort*
you (polite)	o senhor	*oo senyor*
you	você	*vossay*
you too	igualmente	*eegwalment*
youth hostel	albergue de juventude	*albairg duh jooventood*

Z

| zip | fecho de correr | *feshoo duh coorair* |
| zoo | jardim zoológico | *jardeem zoo-oloojeecoo* |

Basic grammar

1 Definite and indefinite articles – **the** and **a**

Apart from verbs and adverbs, words in Portuguese are either masculine or feminine with **o** or **a** being the definite article and **um** or **uma** the indefinite article:

	Singular	Plural	
Masculine	**o**	**os**	- the
Feminine	**a**	**as**	- the
Masculine	**um**	**uns**	- some
Feminine	**uma**	**umas**	- some

e.g. **um homem/uns homens** (a man/some men)

The definite/indefinite article, the noun, verb and adjectives all correspond to each other in terms of number and gender,
e.g. **O homem cansado entrou no banco** (The tired man went into the bank)

2 Plural

Adding an s is usually sufficient:

    casa/casas   (house/houses)

Some nouns form the plural irregularly, such as:

cão > cães	(dog/s)
relação > relações	(relationship/s)
mão > mãos	(hand/s)
doutor > doutores	(doctor/s)
canal > canais	(channel/s)
hotel > hotéis	(hotel/s)
lençol > lençóis	(sheet/s)

3 Personal pronouns

In general **tu** is used for **you** when speaking to close friends, relations and children and pets; o **senhor/a senhora** (or **você**) is used in all other cases:

eu	I
tu	you (familiar)
você	you (semi familiar)
o senhora/a senhora	you (polite)
ele/ela	he/she
nós	we
vós	you (familar)
vocês	you (semi familar)
os senhores/as senhoras	you (polite)
eles/elas	they

4 Possessive pronouns

These correspond to the object they modify:

o meu/a minha (my)	o meu amigo (my friend)
os meus/as minhas (my)	os meus amigos (my friends)
o teu/a tua (your)	o teu irmão (your brother)
os teus/as tuas (your)	os teus irmãos (your brothers)
o seu/a sua (your/his)	o seu marido (your/his/her/ her husband)
os seus/as suas (your/their)	os seus filhos (your/their sons)
dele (his)	a casa dele (his house)
dela (her)	o carro dela (her car)
deles/delas (their)	o neto deles/delas (their grandson)
o nosso/a nossa (our)	o nosso cão (our dog)
os nossos/as nossas (our)	os nossos gatos (our cats)
o vosso/a vossa (your)	o vosso pai (your father)
os vossos/as vossas (your)	os vossos tios (your uncles)